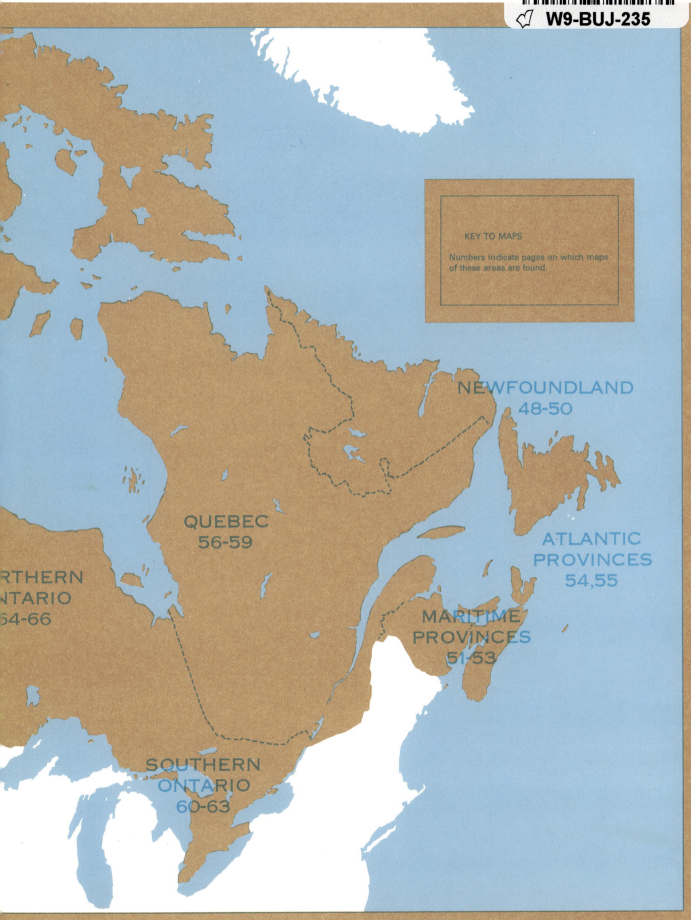

KEY TO MAPS

Numbers indicate pages on which maps
of these areas are found.

NEWFOUNDLAND
48-50

QUEBEC
56-59

ATLANTIC
PROVINCES
54,55

RTHERN
NTARIO
64-66

MARITIME
PROVINCES
51-53

SOUTHERN
ONTARIO
60-63

The Macmillan School Atlas

The Macmillan
SCHOOL ATLAS
Revised Metric Edition

RONALD C. DALY, B.A., M.Ed.

Maps and illustrations by
JOHN R. WALLER

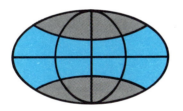

gage EDUCATIONAL PUBLISHING COMPANY
A DIVISION OF CANADA PUBLISHING CORPORATION
TORONTO ONTARIO CANADA

ISBN 0-7715-**8268**-4

7 8 BP 89 88 87 86

Printed and bound in Canada

Contents

The World

People have known for many years that the planet on which they live is a sphere. Although maps can tell us much about its surface, only a globe can show correctly the size, shape, and position of the different areas of land and water.

The distance round the earth is 40 075 km. This is slightly more than 7 times the distance across Canada.

7

The earth's diameter at the equator is 12 757 km. The diameter from north to south is 12 713 km.

The world is not perfectly round but is slightly flattened at the poles. However, since this flattening is so slight and since the earth is so large, we may well think of it as having more or less the shape of a ball.

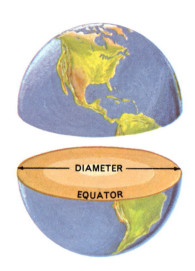

Hemispheres

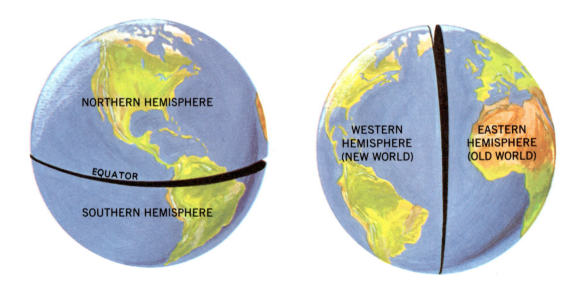

When we look at a globe we see only half of it at one time. This is called a *hemisphere*, which means "half a sphere". No matter how a globe is held, it will show that the earth is divided into two hemispheres, the half that you see and the half that you do not see. These two hemispheres are opposite each other, and by placing them together we are able to make a whole sphere.

By dividing the earth in two at different places we get many different hemispheres. For example, if we cut the earth along the equator, we would separate it into the *Northern Hemisphere* and the *Southern Hemisphere*. If we divided the earth through the Atlantic and Pacific oceans into the Old World and the New World, we would separate it into the *Eastern Hemisphere* and the *Western Hemisphere*.

Two other important hemispheres are the *Land Hemisphere* and the *Water Hemisphere*. The Land Hemisphere contains over ninety per cent of all the land on the earth's surface.

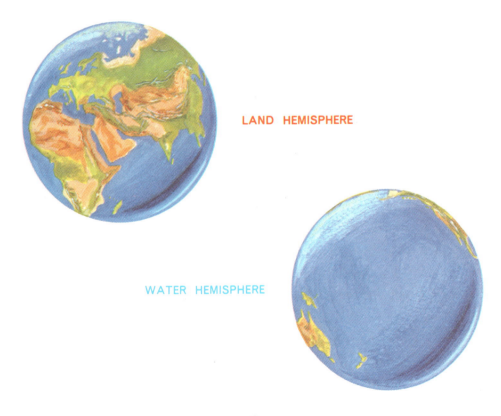

LAND HEMISPHERE

WATER HEMISPHERE

Great Circles

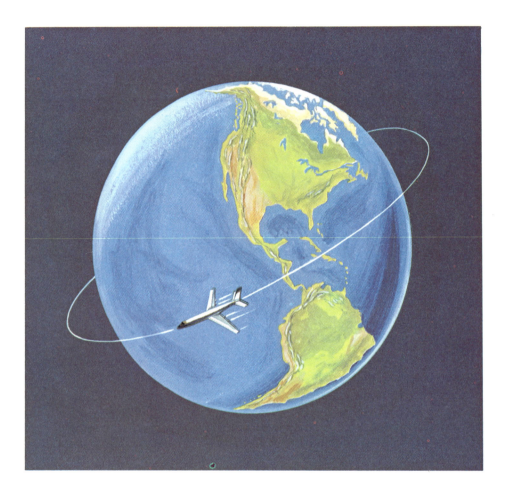

From any place we can draw a circle round the earth that will divide the earth into two hemispheres. Such a line is called a *great circle*.

The shortest distance between any two places on the earth is found on the great circle that joins these two places together. This is called the *great-circle distance*.

Ships often follow great-circle routes to reach their destination. Airplanes can follow these routes over the land as well, unless they are forbidden to do so for political reasons.

Latitude

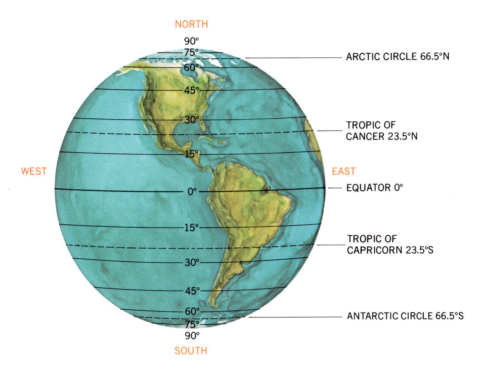

NORTH

90°
75° ——————————— ARCTIC CIRCLE 66.5°N
60°
45°
30° ——————————— TROPIC OF
CANCER 23.5°N
15°

WEST   EAST

0° ——————————— EQUATOR 0°

15° ——————————— TROPIC OF
CAPRICORN 23.5°S
30°
45°
60° ——————————— ANTARCTIC CIRCLE 66.5°S
75°
90°

SOUTH

PARALLELS OF LATITUDE

Any circle can be divided into a number of equal distances known as *degrees*. Every circle, no matter how large or small, has 360 of these degrees. Therefore in half a circle (a hemisphere) there are 180 of them (180°).

The most important dividing line going round the earth from east to west is the *equator*. The position of this imaginary line round the middle of the earth is shown on the globe and is 0° *latitude*. Other lines can be drawn from east to west, parallel to the equator. These lines are called *parallels of latitude*. All places on the same parallel of latitude are an equal distance from the equator. Places north of the equator are in the north latitudes and places south of the equator are in the south latitudes.

11

The numbers on the parallels stand for degrees of latitude. Distance from the equator may be measured in these degrees. No place on the earth's surface can have a latitude greater than 90°. The latitude at the north pole is 90° north of the equator. What would the latitude at the south pole be?

One degree of latitude is equal to about 113 km. Knowing this we can find the distance of any place from the equator if we have its

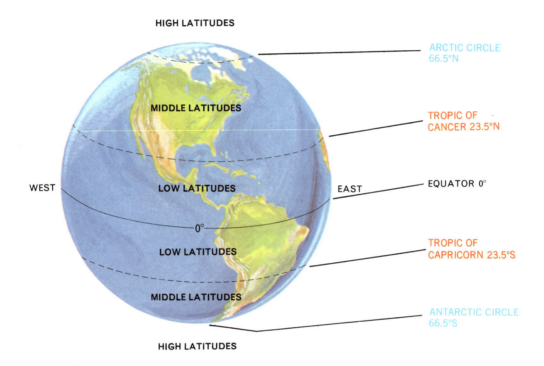

HIGH LATITUDES

ARCTIC CIRCLE
66.5°N

MIDDLE LATITUDES

TROPIC OF
CANCER 23.5°N

WEST   LOW LATITUDES   EAST   EQUATOR 0°

0°

LOW LATITUDES

TROPIC OF
CAPRICORN 23.5°S

MIDDLE LATITUDES

ANTARCTIC CIRCLE
66.5°S

HIGH LATITUDES

latitude. All places on the same parallel are directly east or west of each other. Because of this, the parallels of latitude can help us to find directions as well as distances.

Using parallels of latitude we can divide the earth into *Low Latitudes, Middle Latitudes,* and *High Latitudes.* Zones can be helpful when comparing climates on various parts of the earth's surface. However, you must consider other factors that influence climate before making general statements about a particular place.

Longitude

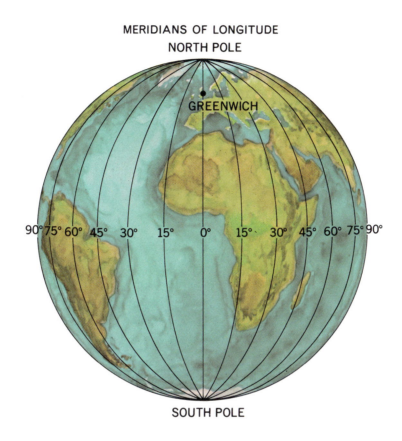

MERIDIANS OF LONGITUDE
NORTH POLE

GREENWICH

90° 75° 60° 45° 30° 15° 0° 15° 30° 45° 60° 75° 90°

SOUTH POLE

To help further in locating places on the earth's surface, a second set of imaginary lines can be drawn. These run from the north pole to the south pole and are called *meridians of longitude*.

Unlike the parallels of latitude, meridians are not parallel to one another but meet at two points—the north pole and the south pole.

The meridian that passes through Greenwich, a suburb of London, England, is 0° and is called the *prime meridian*.

The parallels of latitude and the meridians of longitude appear on most maps and globes as a network of lines, or *grid*. With this

13

grid we can locate accurately any place on earth. We can also compare areas of the earth's surface with the same area on a globe.

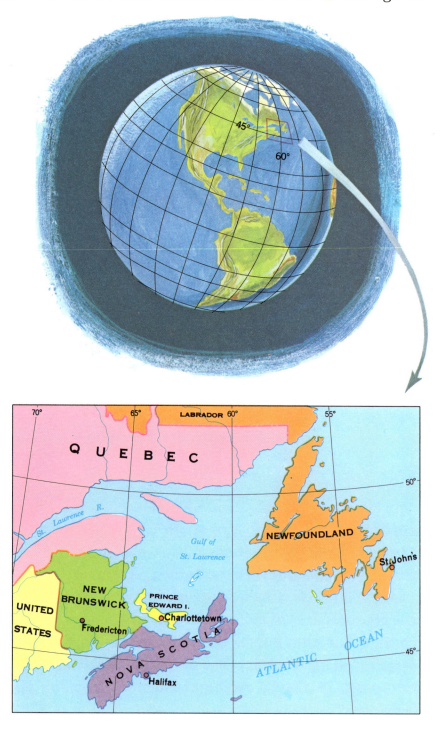

Maps

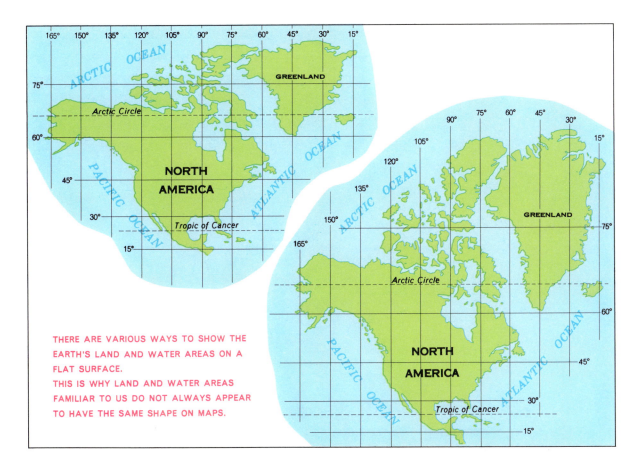

THERE ARE VARIOUS WAYS TO SHOW THE EARTH'S LAND AND WATER AREAS ON A FLAT SURFACE.
THIS IS WHY LAND AND WATER AREAS FAMILIAR TO US DO NOT ALWAYS APPEAR TO HAVE THE SAME SHAPE ON MAPS.

A *map* is a picture of the earth or a part of its surface as seen from above. With the exception of a globe, most maps show the features of the earth on a flat surface. We know that a globe gives us the truest picture of the outline of land and water on the earth's surface, but it is not always as easy to use and handle as a map is. Map-makers have tried different ways of drawing the rounded surface of the earth on a flat piece of paper, but they have always found that they must make some changes in the distances or in the size and shape of the earth's features. A map showing a large area of the earth's surface has more distortion in some of its parts than a map of only a small area.

15

Map-makers use *projections* to draw maps. A projection is a method of flattening the rounded surface of the earth so that it can be drawn on a sheet of paper. To draw a map, the map-maker must transfer the shapes of areas and the grid lines from the globe to the paper. Imagine a sheet of paper placed around a globe and a light placed inside the globe. The light shines through the globe and casts shadows of the outlines of the earth's features and the grid lines onto the paper. By tracing these shadows a map is prepared. More complicated projections are not prepared in this way but are the result of careful mathematical calculations that show how the meridians and parallels should be spaced.

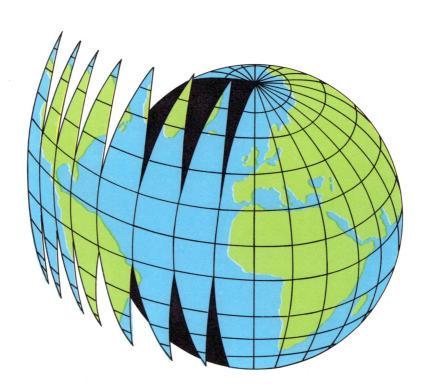

These diagrams show three ways in which the rounded surface of the earth can be represented on a flat surface. In each case the shapes of some areas and some distances are not the same as they are on the globe. If you examine the world maps on pages 26-33, you will see how these distortions appear on different maps.

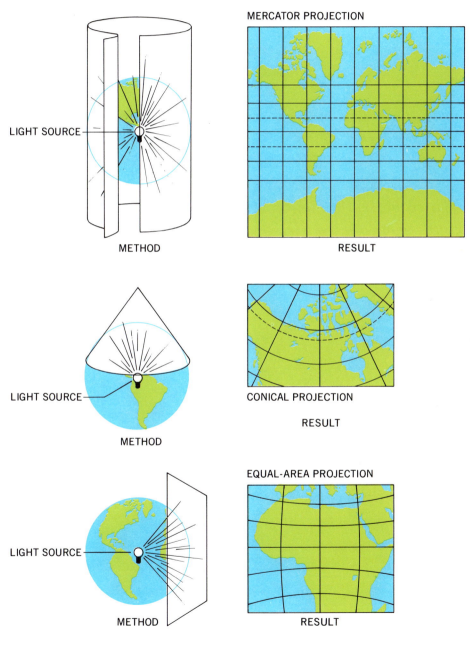

LIGHT SOURCE

METHOD

MERCATOR PROJECTION

RESULT

LIGHT SOURCE

METHOD

CONICAL PROJECTION

RESULT

LIGHT SOURCE

METHOD

EQUAL-AREA PROJECTION

RESULT

17

The Legend and the Scale

Maps are usually grouped according to the kind of information they give. Several kinds of information may be combined on one map.

Many features on a map are shown by special *symbols* and by colours. These are explained in the *legend* of the map. The legend also usually gives the *title* of the map and the *scale*. Every map has its own symbols and colouring. What is used on one map is not always used on another. Colouring in particular often has different meanings. To understand a map we must read it carefully. One of the first steps in map-reading is to look at the legend to see what the symbols mean.

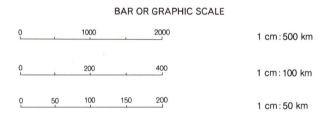

The scale indicates the size of the area shown on the map. In the legend of most maps there is a *bar*, or *graphic*, scale divided into sections. By comparing distances measured on the map with this scale, we can tell what the distances are on the earth.

Each division represents a certain number of kilometres. On different maps the same length of line can stand for different distances. On one map 1 cm might represent 100 km; on another map it might stand for only 50 km.

18

The Direction Sign

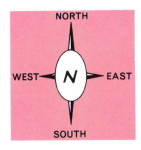

Most maps have a key for finding direction. This is usually an arrow that points toward the north. You must remember, however, that due north is not always at the top of the map.

Elevation

Look at the picture at the right. You can see that the land is not the same everywhere. Some places are only a little above the level of the ocean. These areas are called *lowlands*. Other areas are higher above the ocean level and are called *highlands*.

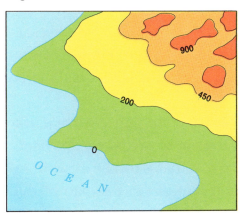

At the left you see a map of the same area. Lines are drawn on the map to join together places where the height of the land is the same. Notice that all the places where the land is 200 m above the level of the ocean are joined together by a line.

All the land that is between 0 and 200 m above sea level is coloured green. The land from 200 m to 450 m is coloured yellow. The land from 450 m to 900 m above sea level is coloured brown. What colour is used to show the land over 900 m?

Night and Day

Once a day the earth makes one complete turn from west to east. It turns round an imaginary line that passes through the centre of the earth from the north pole to the south pole. This line is known as the *axis* of the earth.

We depend on the sun for our heat and our light. As the earth spins on its axis, the part that faces the sun receives heat and light. It is *day* in this part of the earth. The part that is turned away from the sun is cool and is in darkness. It is *night* in this part of the earth.

As we watch the sun in the morning, we say it "rises" in the east. This is not so. The sun does not change its position at all. It is because the earth is turning from west to east that we see the sun "rise" in the east. Our last view of the sun is in the west, as the earth turns away from it.

Time

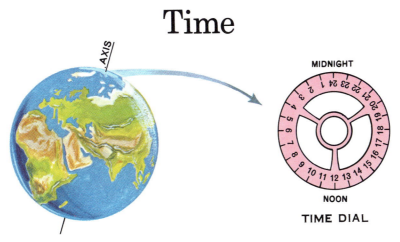

TIME DIAL

All places on Earth do not have noon at the same time. This is due to the earth's shape and to its spinning on its axis. In one day the earth completes one spin (rotation). In twenty-four hours it travels 360 degrees—15 degrees each hour. Noon where you live would be one hour later than in a place fifteen degrees east of you.

To avoid the confusion there would be if every place used its own time, *time zones* have been established. All places within a time zone have the same time. There are twenty-four of these time zones—one for every fifteen degrees.

The borders of time zones do not always follow meridians, but often follow the borders of countries or of provinces and states.

Canada's time zones are shown on the map below.

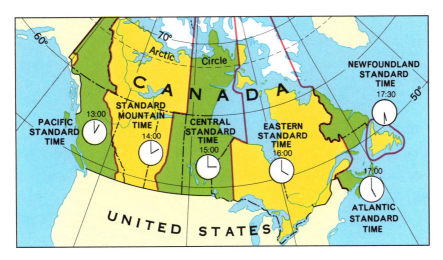

The Change of Seasons

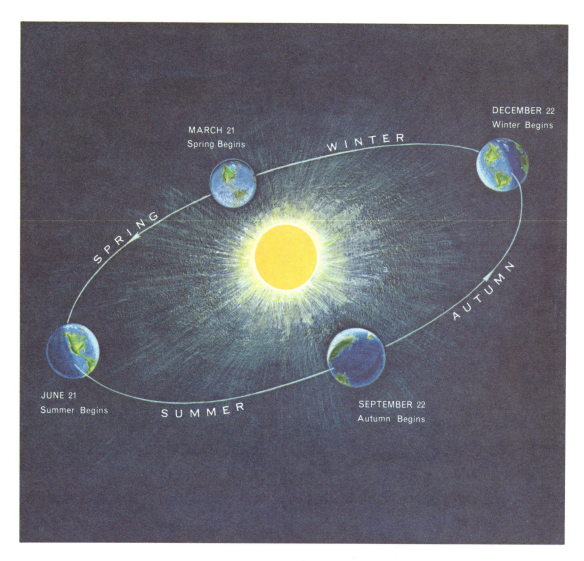

As the earth is turning on its axis, it is also revolving round the sun, in an *orbit*. At the same time, the axis of the earth always points to the North Star. This causes changes in the length of time various places on the earth receive sunlight. It also causes changes in the amount of heat these places receive.

This change in heating is called the change of the *seasons*.

22

The Earth and the Moon

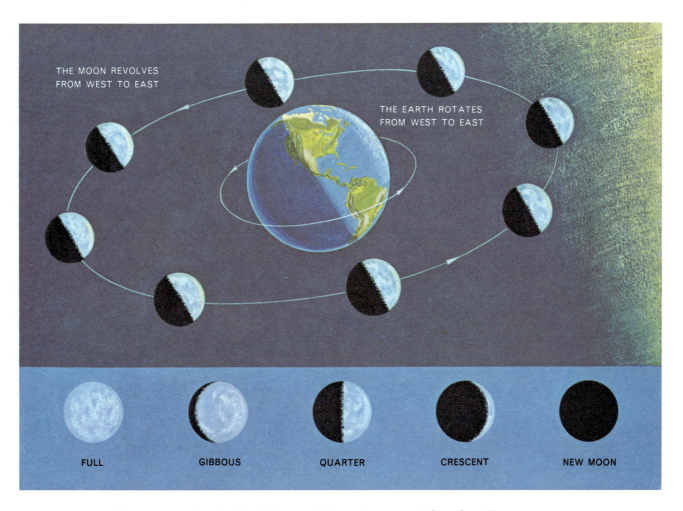

THE MOON REVOLVES FROM WEST TO EAST

THE EARTH ROTATES FROM WEST TO EAST

FULL GIBBOUS QUARTER CRESCENT NEW MOON

The *moon* is the brightest object in our night sky. To a person observing it from the earth, it seems to be as large as the sun. Actually it appears large only because it is closer to us than the sun. The distance from the earth to the moon is about 384 400 km. This is almost 10 times the distance round the earth at its equator.

If you observe the moon closely, you will see that it travels round the earth from west to east. As it does, the amount of it we see lighted changes. These changes are called *phases*.

23

GEOGRAPHIC TERMS
THIS IS A VIEW OF AN AREA THAT INCLUDES THE MAIN FEATURES FOUND ON THE EARTH'S SURFACE; THE GEOGRAPHIC TERMS ARE MARKED ON THESE.

PEAK

M O U N T A I N S

PASS

DIVIDE

VALLEY

SLOPE

River

L O W L A N D S

HILL

PENINSULA

Coastline

Stream

Lake

F O O T H I L L S

Delta

Inlet

Bay

Town

Tributary

Railway

Road

Cape

Strait

Stream

River

B A S I N

CITY

Harbour

Lagoon

Archipelago

Bridge

Bridge

Town

Highway

Reef

Swamp

Canal

P L A I N

Village

Airport

Creek

Road

River Mouth

Beach

Isthmus

Bay

Lighthouse

Cape

Rocks

Strait

Gulf

Bluff

Headland

ISLAND

Rocks

S E A

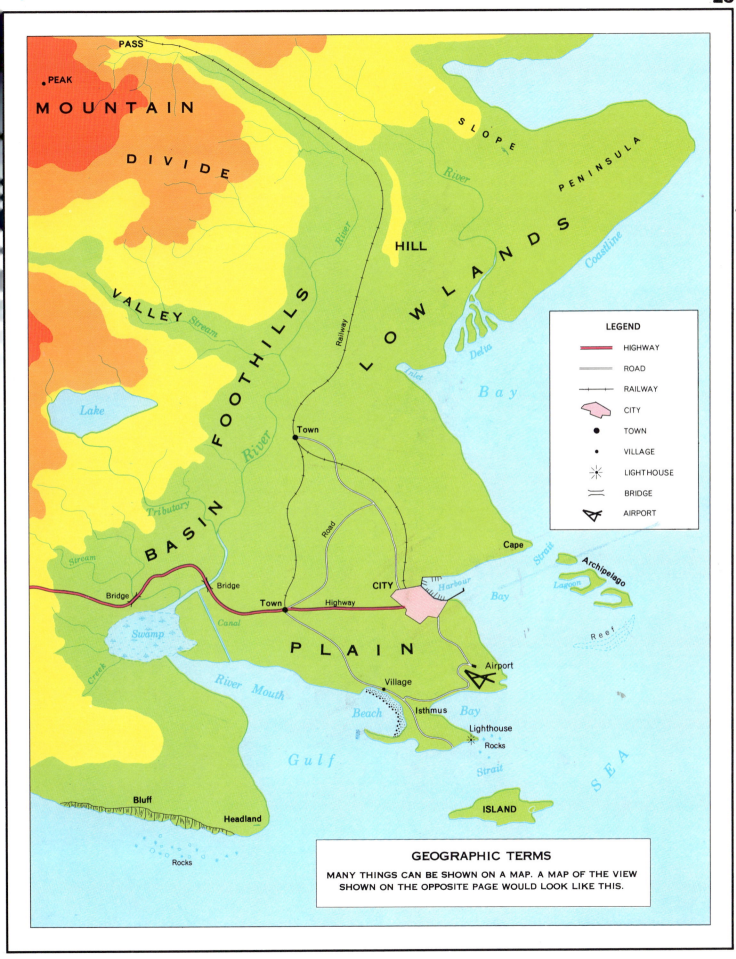

LEGEND

▬▬▬	HIGHWAY
═══	ROAD
┼┼┼┼	RAILWAY
⬠	CITY
●	TOWN
•	VILLAGE
✳	LIGHTHOUSE
╪	BRIDGE
◁	AIRPORT

GEOGRAPHIC TERMS

MANY THINGS CAN BE SHOWN ON A MAP. A MAP OF THE VIEW
SHOWN ON THE OPPOSITE PAGE WOULD LOOK LIKE THIS.

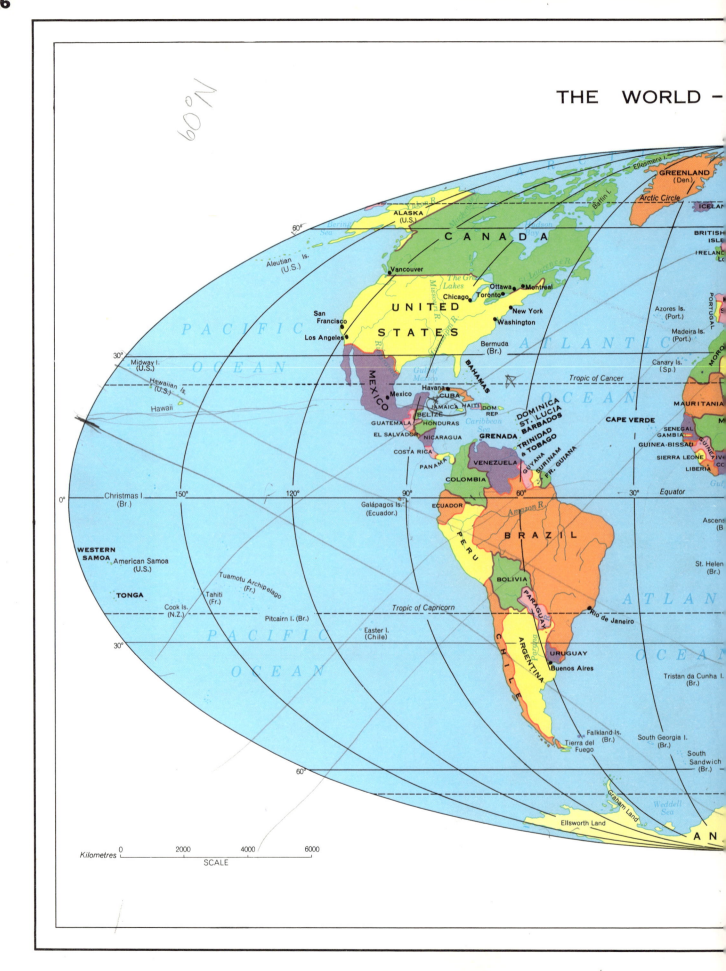

60°N

GREENLAND
(Den.)

Arctic Circle

ICELAN

Ellesmere I.

ALASKA
(U.S.)

Baffin I.

BRITISH
ISLE

IRELAND

Bering
Sea

60°

C A N A D A

Hudson
Bay

Aleutian Is.
(U.S.)

St. Lawrence R.

Vancouver

The Gre
Lakes

Azores Is.
(Port.)

PORTUGAL

Ottawa
Montreal
Chicago
Toronto

U N I T E D

San
Francisco

Madeira Is.
(Port.)

MORO

S T A T E S

New York
Washington

P A C I F I C

Los Angeles

A T L A N T I C

30°

Bermuda
(Br.)

Canary Is.
(Sp.)

Midway I.
(U.S.)

O C E A N

Tropic of Cancer

MAURITANIA

Hawaiian Is.
(U.S.)

MEXICO

Havana
CUBA

BAHAMAS

O C E A N

CAPE VERDE

Hawaii

Mexico

JAMAICA HAITI
DOM
REP

DOMINICA
ST. LUCIA
BARBADOS

SENEGAL
GAMBIA

BELIZE

GUATEMALA
HONDURAS

GRENADA

TRINIDAD
& TOBAGO

GUINEA-BISSAU

GUINEA

EL SALVADOR
NICARAGUA

SIERRA LEONE
LIBERIA

CO

COSTA RICA

VENEZUELA

GUYANA
SURINAM
FR. GUIANA

Gul

PANAMA

0°

Christmas I.
(Br.)

150°

120°

90°

COLOMBIA

60°

30°

Equator

Galápagos Is.
(Ecuador.)

ECUADOR

Amazon R.

Ascens
(B

WESTERN
SAMOA

American Samoa
(U.S.)

P
E
R
U

B R A Z I L

St. Helen
(Br.)

TONGA

Tahiti
(Fr.)

Tuamotu Archipelago
(Fr.)

BOLIVIA

Rio de Janeiro

A T L A N

Cook Is.
(N.Z.)

Pitcairn I. (Br.)

Tropic of Capricorn

PARAGUAY

Easter I.
(Chile)

Tristan da Cunha I.
(Br.)

30°

URUGUAY

C
H
I
L
E

A
R
G
E
N
T
I
N
A

Buenos Aires

South Georgia I.
(Br.)

P A C I F I C

O C E A N

Falkland Is.
(Br.)

South
Sandwich
(Br.)

Tierra del
Fuego

60°

Graham Land

Weddell
Sea

Ellsworth Land

A N

POLITICAL DIVISIONS

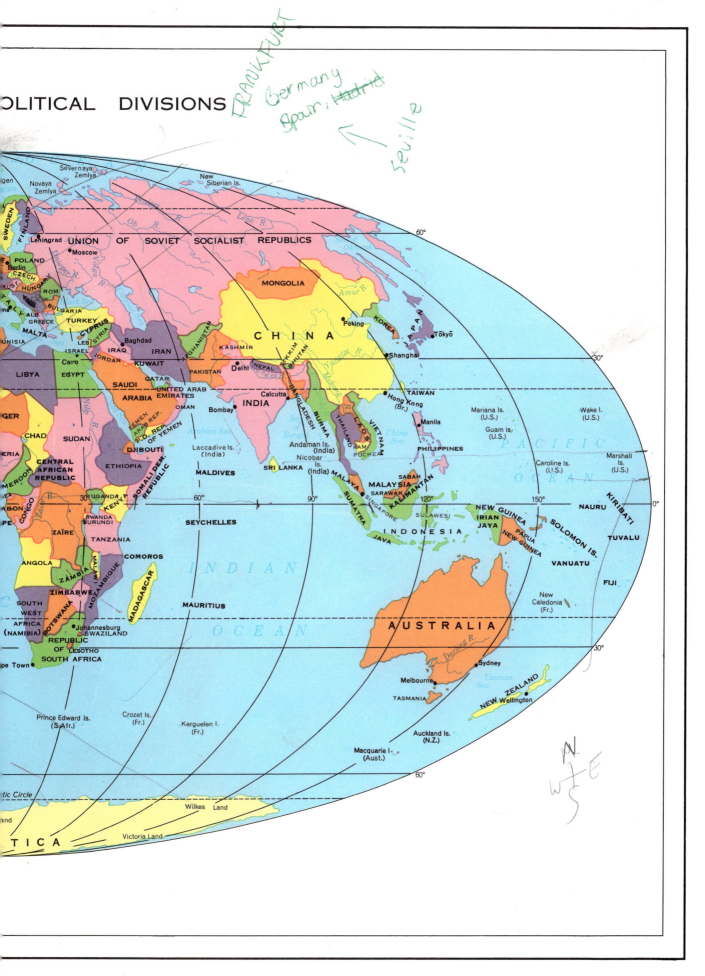

FRANKFURT
Germany
Spain, Madrid
Seville

N
W E
S

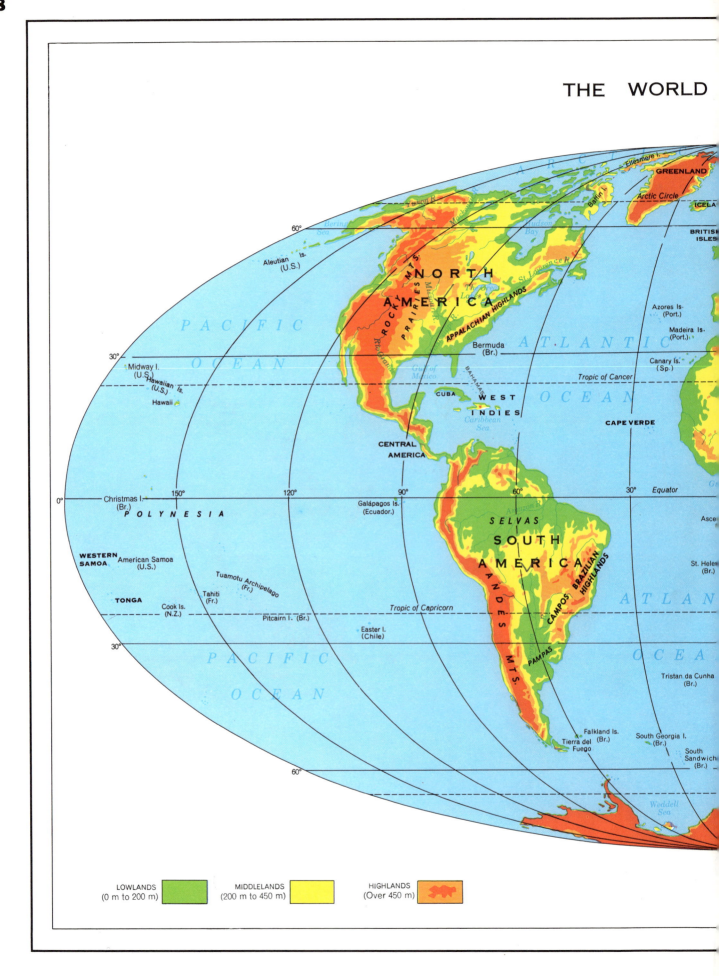

LOWLANDS
(0 m to 200 m)

MIDDLELANDS
(200 m to 450 m)

HIGHLANDS
(Over 450 m)

ANDFORMS – RELIEF

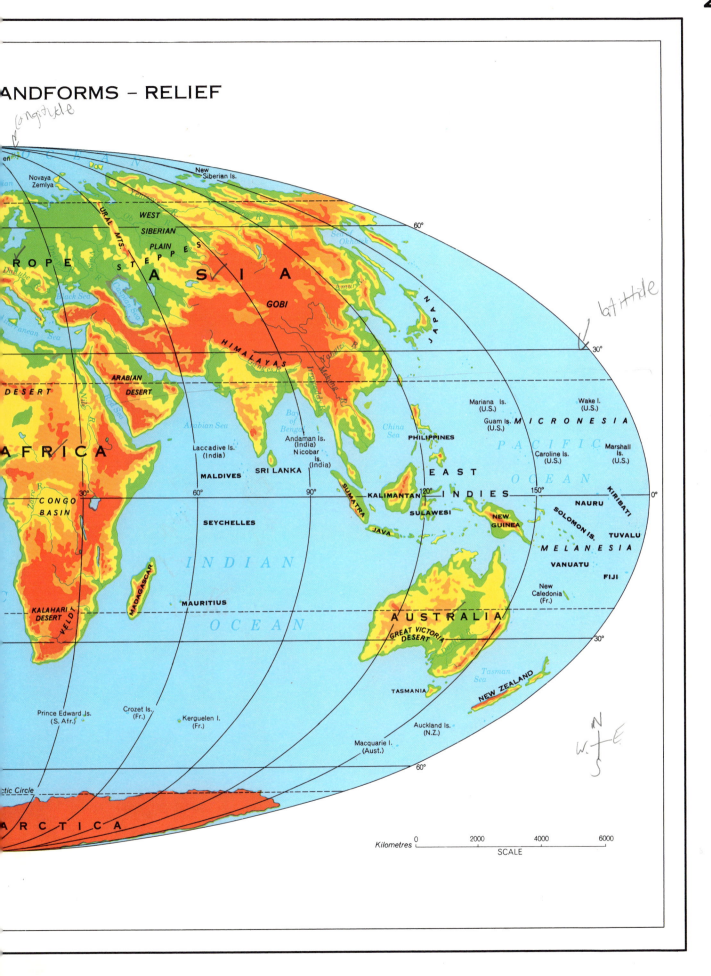

longitude

latitude

ARCTIC OCEAN

Novaya Zemlya

New Siberian Is.

URAL MTS.

WEST SIBERIAN PLAIN

STEPPES

ROPE

Danube

Black Sea

Caspian Sea

Mediterranean Sea

A S I A

GOBI

Amur R.

Sea of Okhotsk

HIMALAYAS

Yangtze R.

Mekong R.

60°

JAPAN

30°

ARABIAN DESERT

DESERT

Red Sea

ARABIAN DESERT

Arabian Sea

Bay of Bengal

China Sea

Mariana Is. (U.S.)

Wake I. (U.S.)

Guam Is. (U.S.)

M I C R O N E S I A

A F R I C A

Laccadive Is. (India)

Andaman Is. (India)

Nicobar Is. (India)

PHILIPPINES

P A C I F I C

Caroline Is. (U.S.)

Marshall Is. (U.S.)

MALDIVES

SRI LANKA

E A S T

O C E A N

Congo Zaire R.

CONGO BASIN

30°

60°

90°

SUMATRA

KALIMANTAN

120°

I N D I E S

150°

0°

KIRIBATI

NAURU

SEYCHELLES

SULAWESI

JAVA

NEW GUINEA

SOLOMON IS.

TUVALU

M E L A N E S I A

VANUATU

FIJI

I N D I A N

New Caledonia (Fr.)

KALAHARI DESERT

VELDT

MADAGASCAR

MAURITIUS

O C E A N

A U S T R A L I A

GREAT VICTORIA DESERT

30°

Tasman Sea

TASMANIA

NEW ZEALAND

Prince Edward Is. (S. Afr.)

Crozet Is. (Fr.)

Kerguelen I. (Fr.)

Auckland Is. (N.Z.)

Macquarie I. (Aust.)

60°

ctic Circle

ARCTICA

N

W E

S

| Kilometres | 0 | 2000 | 4000 | 6000 |

SCALE

30

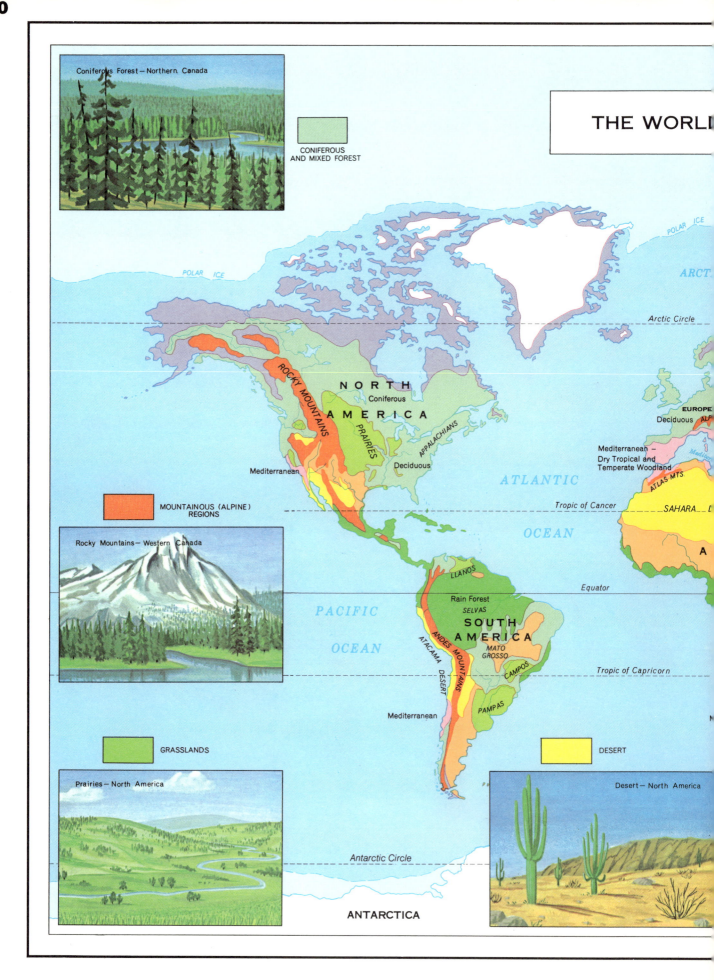

Coniferous Forest — Northern Canada

CONIFEROUS
AND MIXED FOREST

THE WORLD

POLAR ICE

ARCT

Arctic Circle

EUROPE
Deciduous ALP

ROCKY MOUNTAINS

NORTH
AMERICA

Coniferous

PRAIRIES

APPALACHIANS

Deciduous

Mediterranean

Mediterranean —
Dry Tropical and
Temperate Woodland

ATLANTIC

ATLAS MTS.

SAHARA

Tropic of Cancer

OCEAN

A

MOUNTAINOUS (ALPINE)
REGIONS

Rocky Mountains — Western Canada

PACIFIC

LLANOS

Equator

Rain Forest
SELVAS

SOUTH
AMERICA

MATO
GROSSO

ANDES MOUNTAINS

ATACAMA
DESERT

CAMPOS

Tropic of Capricorn

OCEAN

Mediterranean

PAMPAS

GRASSLANDS

DESERT

Prairies — North America

Desert — North America

Antarctic Circle

ANTARCTICA

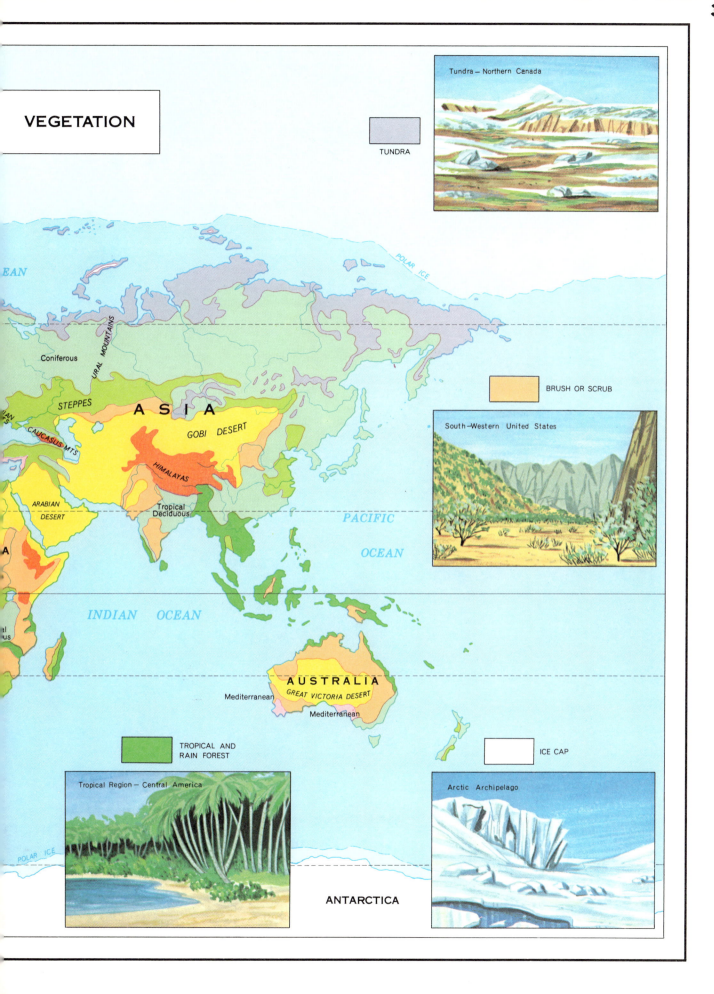

VEGETATION

TUNDRA

Tundra — Northern Canada

BRUSH OR SCRUB

South-Western United States

POLAR ICE

Coniferous

URAL MOUNTAINS

STEPPES

A S I A

GOBI DESERT

CAUCASUS MTS

HIMALAYAS

ARABIAN
DESERT

Tropical
Deciduous

PACIFIC

OCEAN

INDIAN OCEAN

AUSTRALIA
GREAT VICTORIA DESERT

Mediterranean

Mediterranean

TROPICAL AND
RAIN FOREST

ICE CAP

Tropical Region — Central America

Arctic Archipelago

POLAR ICE

ANTARCTICA

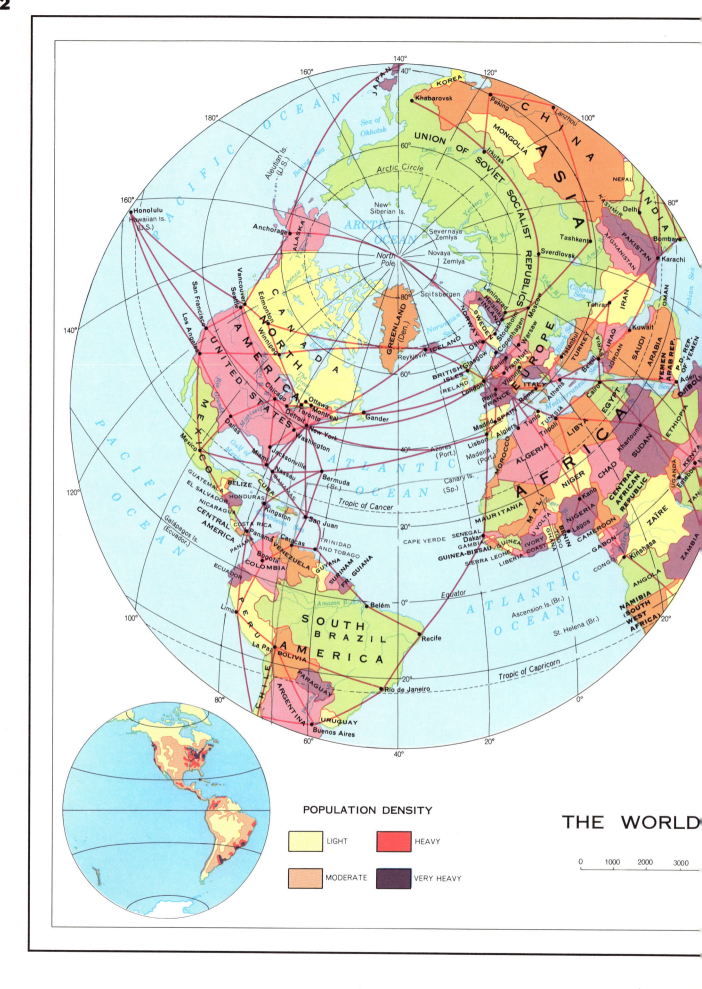

POPULATION DENSITY

LIGHT

HEAVY

MODERATE

VERY HEAVY

THE WORLD

0   1000   2000   3000

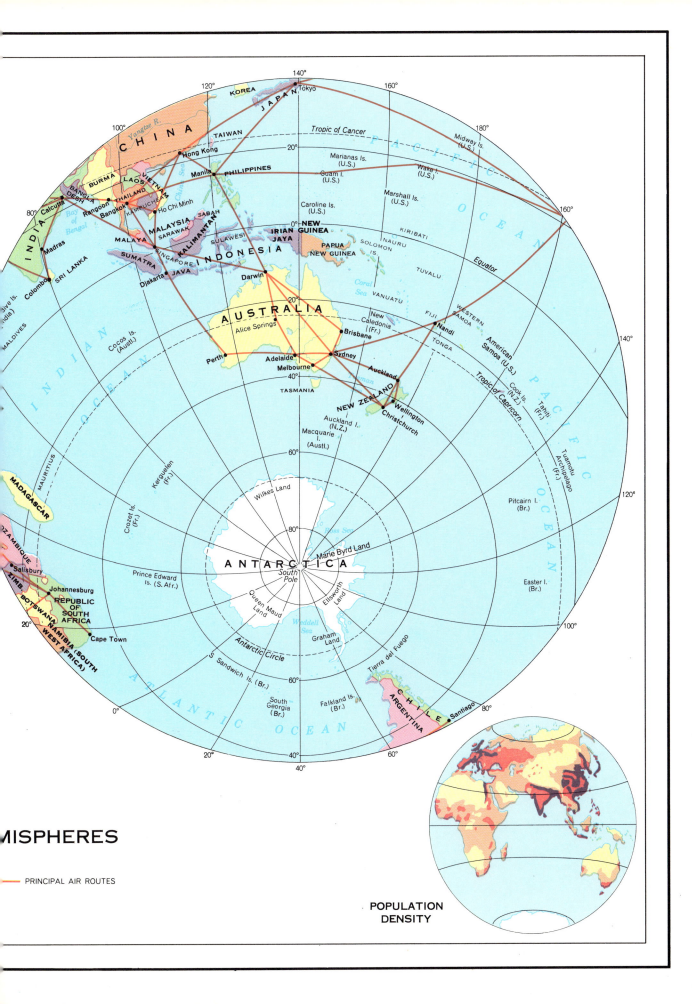

Tropic of Cancer

CHINA

KOREA

JAPAN Tokyo

TAIWAN

Midway Is. (U.S.)

Hong Kong

BURMA LAOS VIETNAM Manila PHILIPPINES

Marianas Is. (U.S.)

Wake I. (U.S.)

BANGLA DESH THAILAND

Guam I. (U.S.)

Marshall Is. (U.S.)

Calcutta Rangoon Bangkok KAMPUCHEA Ho Chi Minh

Caroline Is. (U.S.)

INDIA

Madras

MALAYSIA SABAH SARAWAK

KIRIBATI

NEW GUINEA

SRI LANKA

MALAYA Singapore KALIMANTAN

IRIAN JAYA

NAURU

Colombo

SUMATRA Djakarta JAVA INDONESIA

PAPUA NEW GUINEA

SOLOMON IS.

TUVALU

Maldive Is. (India)

Darwin

Equator

MALDIVES

VANUATU

Coral Sea

INDIAN

AUSTRALIA

Alice Springs

New Caledonia (Fr.)

FIJI

WESTERN SAMOA

Nandi

American Samoa (U.S.)

OCEAN

Cocos Is. (Austl.)

Brisbane

TONGA

Perth

Adelaide Melbourne

Sydney

Auckland

Cook Is. (N.Z.)

Tahiti (Fr.)

MAURITIUS

TASMANIA

Wellington Christchurch

NEW ZEALAND

Tropic of Capricorn

Tuamotu Archipelago (Fr.)

MADAGASCAR

Kerguelen (Fr.)

Auckland I. (N.Z.)

Macquarie I. (Austl.)

PACIFIC OCEAN

Pitcairn I. (Br.)

Crozet Is. (Fr.)

Wilkes Land

MOZAMBIQUE

Salisbury

Prince Edward Is. (S. Afr.)

Ross Sea

Marie Byrd Land

Easter I. (Br.)

ANTARCTICA

South Pole

ZIMB

Johannesburg

Queen Maud Land

Ellsworth Land

BOTSWANA

NAMIBIA (SOUTH WEST AFRICA)

REPUBLIC OF SOUTH AFRICA

Cape Town

Antarctic Circle

Weddell Sea

Graham Land

S. Sandwich Is. (Br.)

ATLANTIC OCEAN

Tierra del Fuego

ARGENTINA CHILE

Santiago

South Georgia (Br.)

Falkland Is. (Br.)

MISPHERES

—— PRINCIPAL AIR ROUTES

POPULATION DENSITY

NORTH AMERICA
POLITICAL DIVISIONS

LEGEND

- CAPITAL CITIES
- PROVINCIAL CAPITALS
- INTERNATIONAL BOUNDARIES
- STATE AND PROVINCIAL BOUNDARIES

Kilometres 0 400 800 1200
SCALE

NORTH AMERICA
LANDFORMS
RELIEF

LEGEND

LOWLANDS
(0 m to 200 m)

MIDDLELANDS
(200 m to 450 m)

HIGHLANDS
(Over 450 m)

Kilometres 0   400   800   1200
SCALE

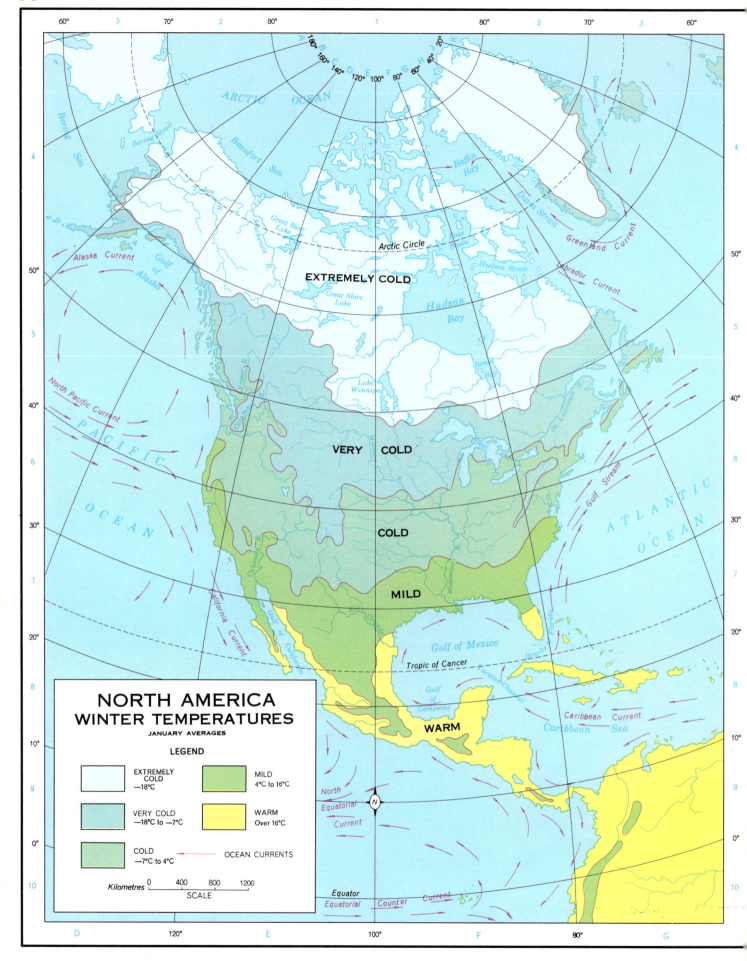

ARCTIC OCEAN

EXTREMELY COLD

VERY COLD

COLD

MILD

WARM

PACIFIC OCEAN

ATLANTIC OCEAN

Arctic Circle

Tropic of Cancer

Equator

Alaska Current
North Pacific Current
California Current
Gulf of Alaska
Bering Sea
Beaufort Sea
Great Bear Lake
Great Slave Lake
Lake Winnipeg
Hudson Bay
James Bay
Hudson Strait
Baffin Bay
Davis Strait
Denmark Strait
Greenland Current
Labrador Current
Gulf Stream
Gulf of Mexico
Gulf of Campeche
Gulf of California
Yucatan Channel
Caribbean Sea
Caribbean Current
North Equatorial Current
Equatorial Counter Current

NORTH AMERICA
WINTER TEMPERATURES
JANUARY AVERAGES

LEGEND

	EXTREMELY COLD —18°C		MILD 4°C to 16°C
	VERY COLD —18°C to —7°C		WARM Over 16°C
	COLD —7°C to 4°C	→	OCEAN CURRENTS

Kilometres 0 400 800 1200
SCALE

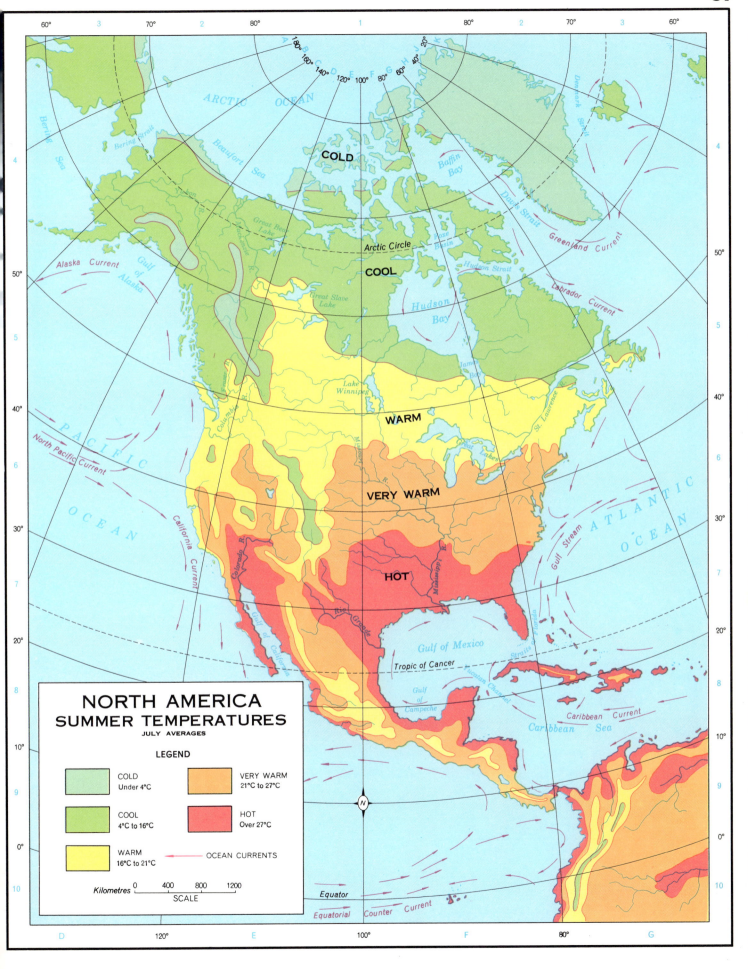

NORTH AMERICA
SUMMER TEMPERATURES
JULY AVERAGES

LEGEND

COLD
Under 4°C

COOL
4°C to 16°C

WARM
16°C to 21°C

VERY WARM
21°C to 27°C

HOT
Over 27°C

→ OCEAN CURRENTS

Kilometres
0 400 800 1200
SCALE

COLD

COOL

WARM

VERY WARM

HOT

ARCTIC OCEAN

Bering Sea

Beaufort Sea

Baffin Bay

Denmark Strait

Arctic Circle

Davis Strait

Greenland Current

Hudson Strait

Alaska Current

Gulf of Alaska

Great Bear Lake

Foxe Basin

Labrador Current

Great Slave Lake

Hudson Bay

James Bay

Lake Winnipeg

Columbia R.

Lake Winnipeg

Great Lakes

St. Lawrence

PACIFIC OCEAN

North Pacific Current

California Current

Missouri R.

Mississippi R.

Gulf Stream

ATLANTIC OCEAN

Colorado R.

Rio Grande

Gulf of California

Gulf of Mexico

Tropic of Cancer

Florida

Straits

Yucatan Channel

Gulf of Campeche

Caribbean Current

Caribbean Sea

N

Equator

Equatorial Counter Current

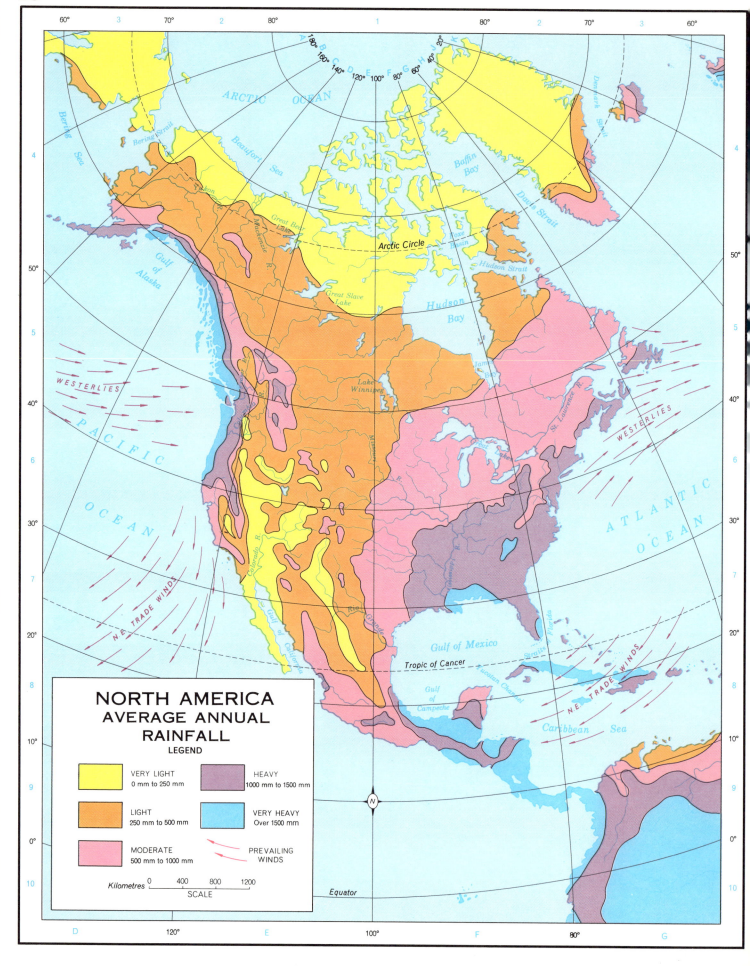

NORTH AMERICA
AVERAGE ANNUAL RAINFALL
LEGEND

	VERY LIGHT 0 mm to 250 mm		HEAVY 1000 mm to 1500 mm
	LIGHT 250 mm to 500 mm		VERY HEAVY Over 1500 mm
	MODERATE 500 mm to 1000 mm		PREVAILING WINDS

Kilometres 0   400   800   1200
SCALE

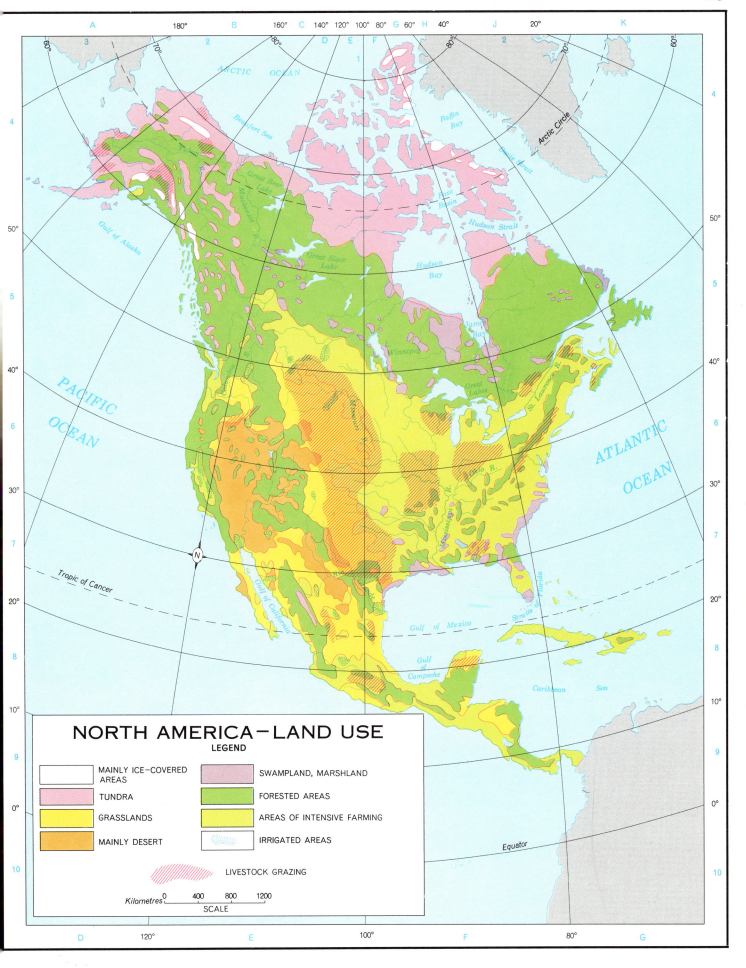

NORTH AMERICA—LAND USE

LEGEND

☐ MAINLY ICE-COVERED AREAS	SWAMPLAND, MARSHLAND
TUNDRA	FORESTED AREAS
GRASSLANDS	AREAS OF INTENSIVE FARMING
MAINLY DESERT	IRRIGATED AREAS
	LIVESTOCK GRAZING

Kilometres 0   400   800   1200
SCALE

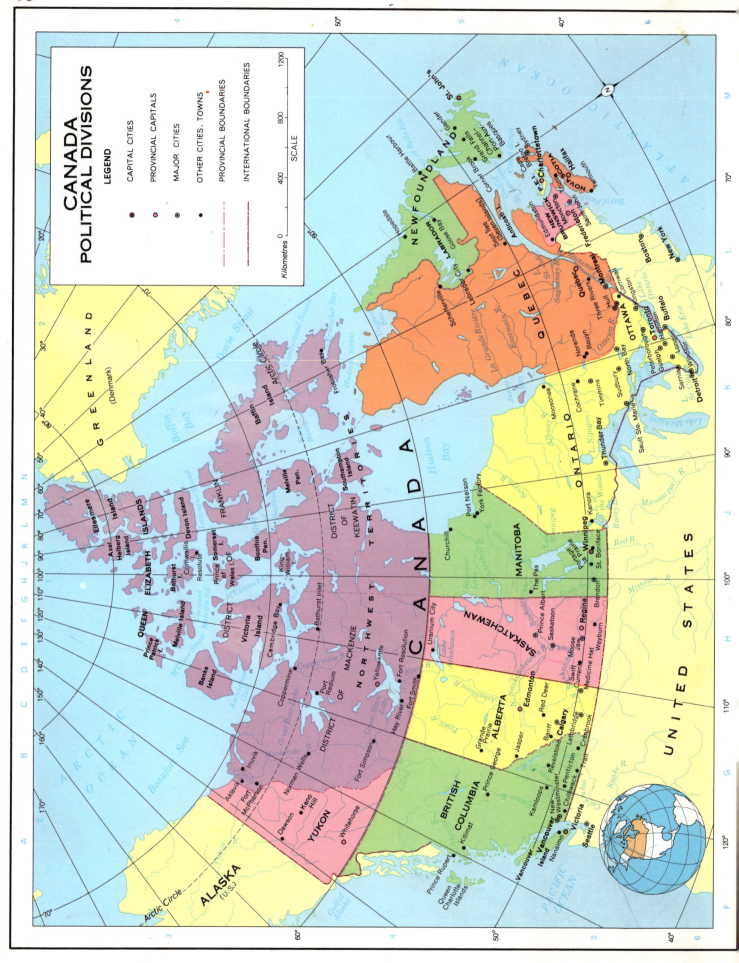

CANADA POLITICAL DIVISIONS

LEGEND

CAPITAL CITIES
PROVINCIAL CAPITALS
MAJOR CITIES
OTHER CITIES, TOWNS
PROVINCIAL BOUNDARIES
INTERNATIONAL BOUNDARIES

SCALE

1200
800
400
0
Kilometres

GREENLAND (Denmark)

ARCTIC OCEAN

NEWFOUNDLAND

LABRADOR

QUEBEC

QUEEN ELIZABETH ISLANDS

Ellesmere Island

Axel Heiberg Island

Devon Island

Cornwallis

Resolute

Bathurst Island

Melville Island

Prince Patrick I.

Banks Island

Victoria Island

King William I.

Boothia Pen.

Melville Pen.

Southampton Island

Baffin Island

Prince of Wales I.

Somerset I.

FRANKLIN

DISTRICT OF MACKENZIE

DISTRICT OF KEEWATIN

NORTHWEST TERRITORIES

CANADA

Coppermine

Port Radium

Cambridge Bay

Bathurst Inlet

Yellowknife

Hay River

Fort Resolution

Fort Smith

Fort Simpson

Norman Wells

Inuvik

Aklavik

Fort McPherson

Dawson

Keno Hill

Whitehorse

YUKON

ALASKA (U.S.)

Queen Charlotte Islands

Prince Rupert

Kitimat

BRITISH COLUMBIA

Prince George

Kamloops

Revelstoke

Penticton

Chilliwack

New Westminster

Vancouver

Victoria

Nanaimo

Vancouver Island

Seattle

PACIFIC OCEAN

Grande Prairie

Jasper

Banff

Calgary

Cranbrook

Trail

Lethbridge

Red Deer

Edmonton

ALBERTA

Medicine Hat

Uranium City

Lake Athabasca

Prince Albert

Saskatoon

Moose Jaw

Swift Current

Regina

Weyburn

SASKATCHEWAN

Churchill

Port Nelson

York Factory

The Pas

Brandon

Winnipeg

St. Boniface

MANITOBA

Kenora

Lake of the Woods

Thunder Bay

L. Nipigon

Sault Ste. Marie

Sudbury

North Bay

Timmins

Cochrane

Moosonee

Albany R.

ONTARIO

Hudson Bay

James Bay

Frobisher Bay

Arctic Circle

Hopedale

Battle Harbour

Belle Isle

Gander

Grand Falls

Corner Brook

St. John's

Channel Port aux Basques

Sydney

NOVA SCOTIA

Yarmouth

Halifax

Charlottetown

P.E.I.

NEW BRUNSWICK

Fredericton

Moncton

Edmundston

Anticosti

Schefferville

Labrador City

Seven Islands

Baie Comeau

Saguenay R.

Rimouski

Quebec

Three Rivers

Montreal

Hull

OTTAWA

Cornwall

Kingston

Peterborough

Toronto

Hamilton

London

Windsor

Sarnia

Detroit

Buffalo

New York

Boston

Noranda

Rouyn

ATLANTIC OCEAN

UNITED STATES

Lake Superior

Lake Michigan

Lake Huron

Lake Ontario

Lake Erie

Mississippi R.

Missouri R.

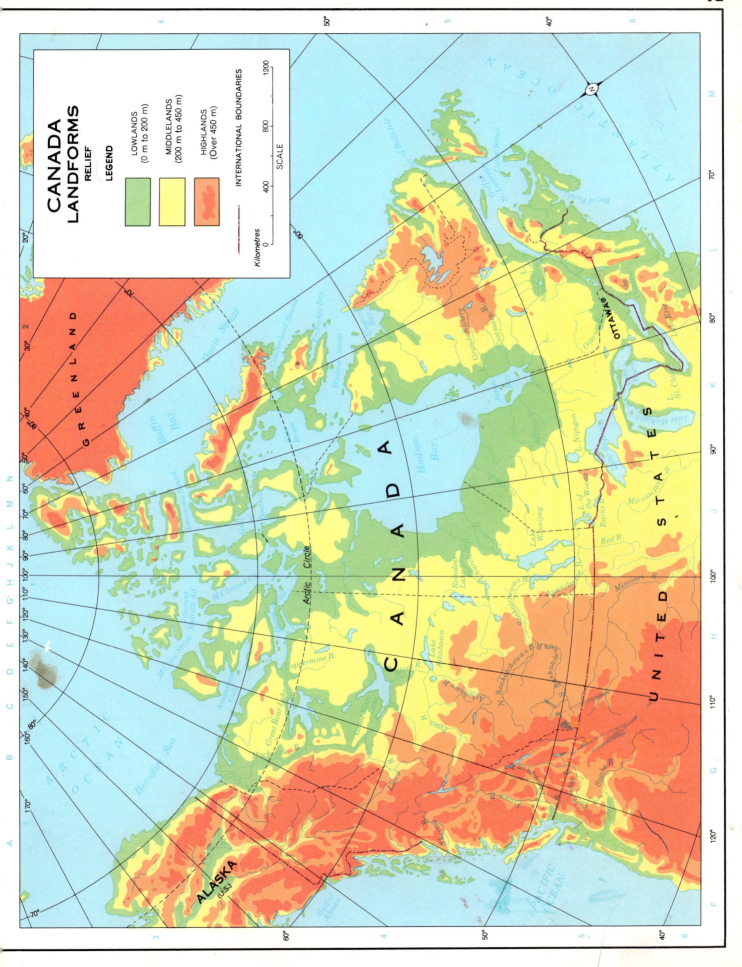

CANADA LANDFORMS

RELIEF

LEGEND

LOWLANDS
(0 m to 200 m)

MIDDLELANDS
(200 m to 450 m)

HIGHLANDS
(Over 450 m)

INTERNATIONAL BOUNDARIES

SCALE

1200

800

400

0

Kilometres

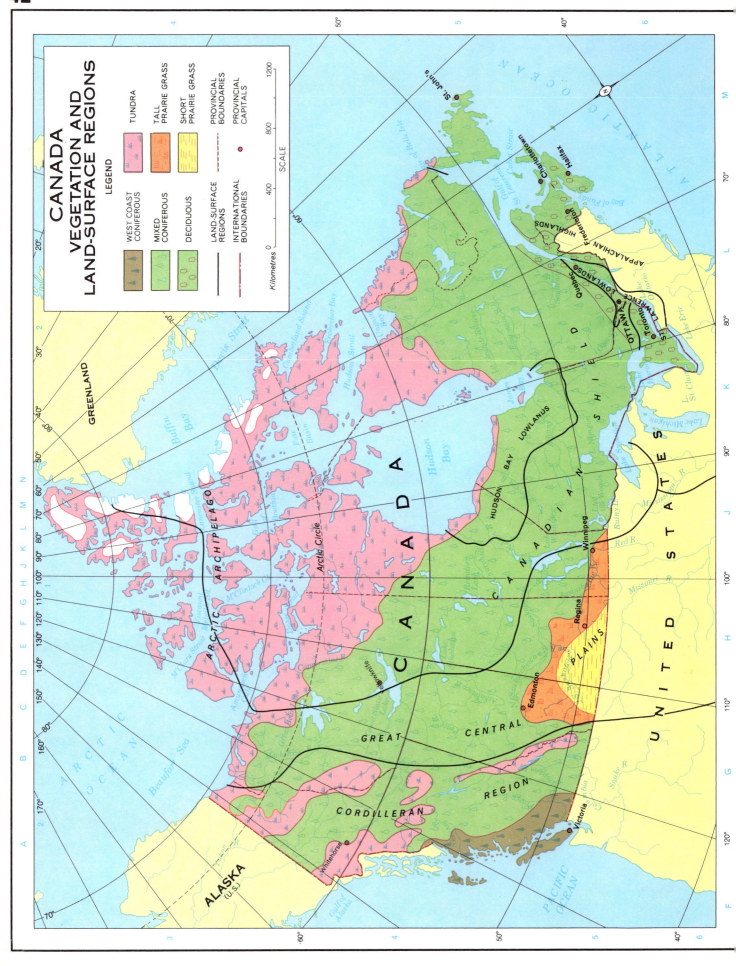

CANADA
VEGETATION AND
LAND-SURFACE REGIONS

LEGEND

WEST COAST CONIFEROUS
MIXED CONIFEROUS
DECIDUOUS

TUNDRA
TALL PRAIRIE GRASS
SHORT PRAIRIE GRASS

LAND-SURFACE REGIONS
INTERNATIONAL BOUNDARIES

PROVINCIAL BOUNDARIES
PROVINCIAL CAPITALS

SCALE

Kilometres

0   400   800   1200

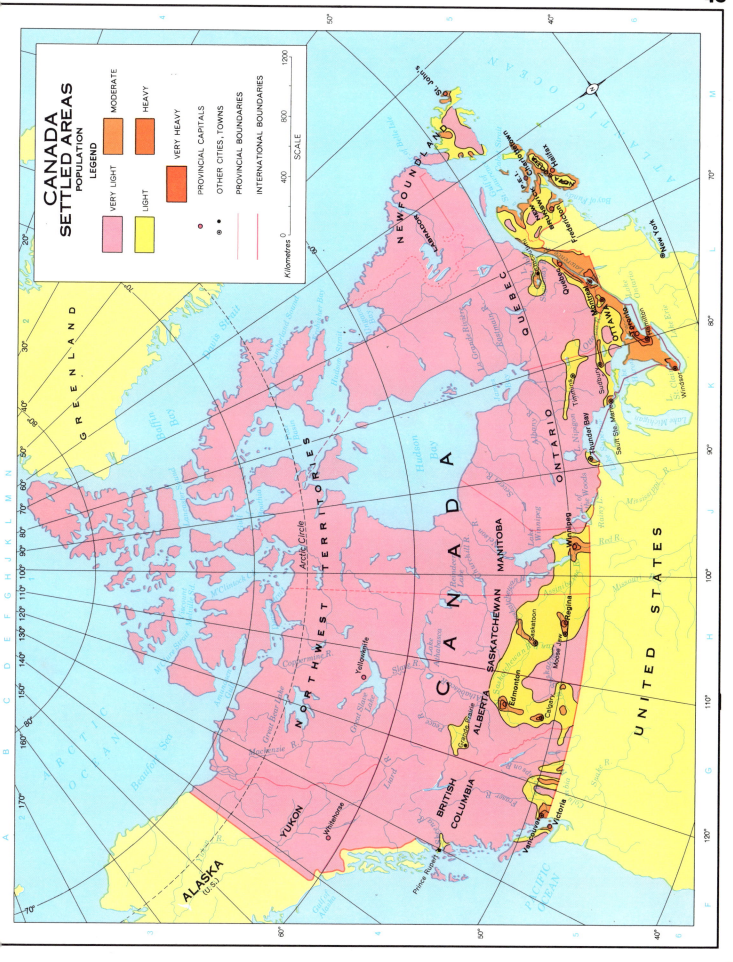

CANADA
SETTLED AREAS
POPULATION
LEGEND

MODERATE

HEAVY

VERY LIGHT

LIGHT

VERY HEAVY

PROVINCIAL CAPITALS

OTHER CITIES, TOWNS

PROVINCIAL BOUNDARIES

INTERNATIONAL BOUNDARIES

SCALE

Kilometres

0   400   800   1200

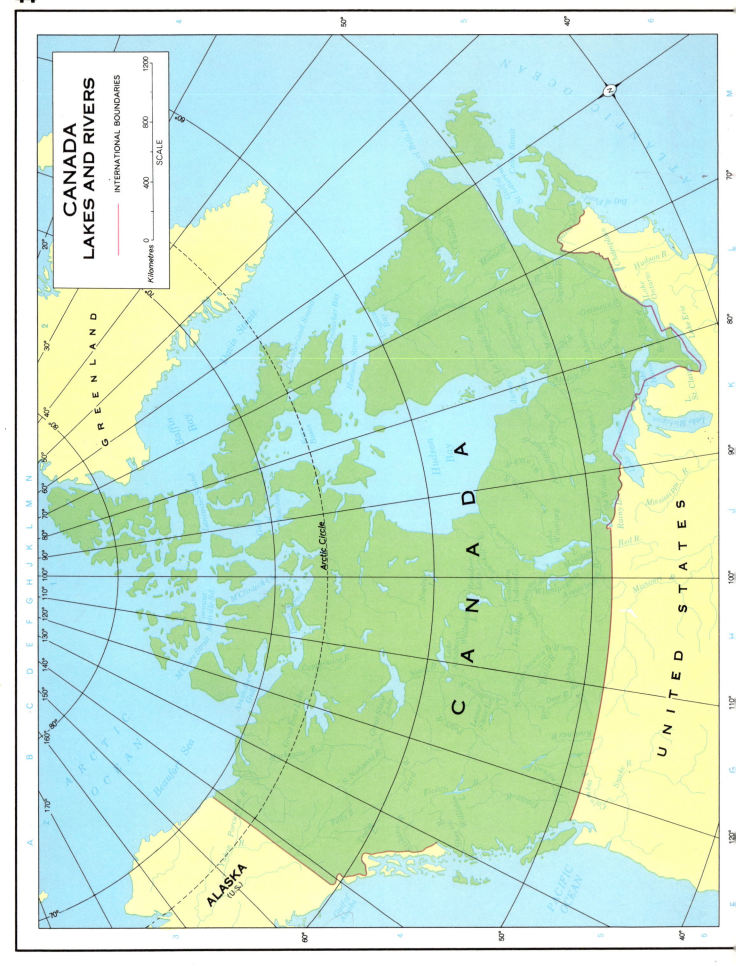

CANADA
LAKES AND RIVERS

INTERNATIONAL BOUNDARIES

SCALE

Kilometres

GREENLAND

ARCTIC OCEAN

ATLANTIC OCEAN

Baffin Bay

Beaufort Sea

ALASKA (U.S.)

Arctic Circle

C A N A D A

Hudson Bay

U N I T E D   S T A T E S

PACIFIC OCEAN

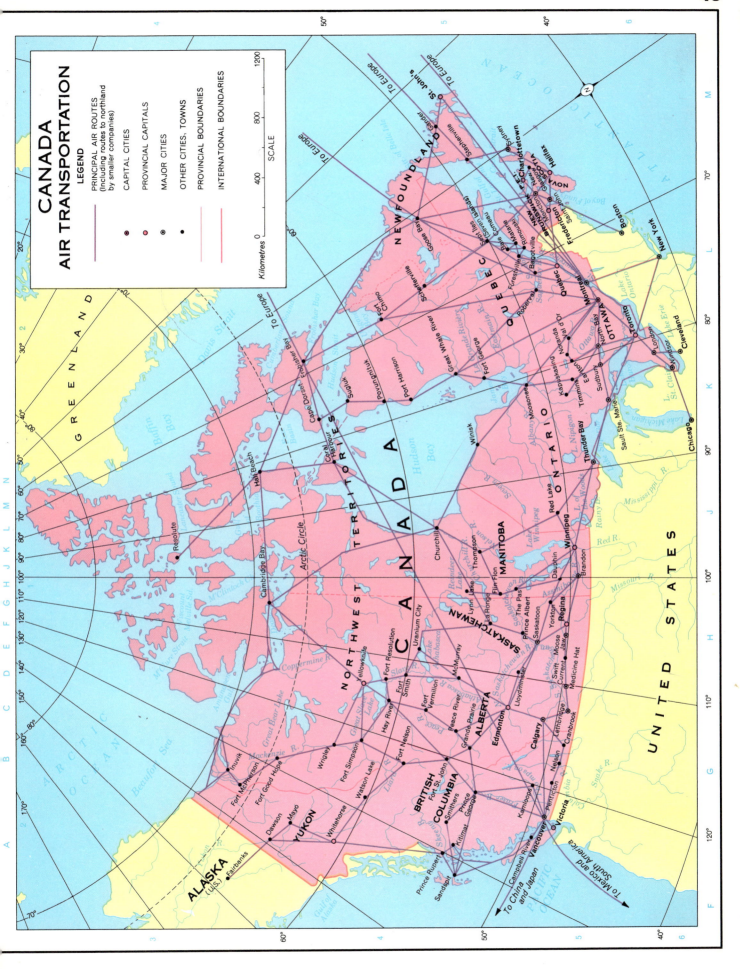

CANADA
AIR TRANSPORTATION

LEGEND

PRINCIPAL AIR ROUTES
(Including routes to northland
by smaller companies)

CAPITAL CITIES

PROVINCIAL CAPITALS

MAJOR CITIES

OTHER CITIES, TOWNS

PROVINCIAL BOUNDARIES

INTERNATIONAL BOUNDARIES

SCALE

Kilometres

0   400   800   1200

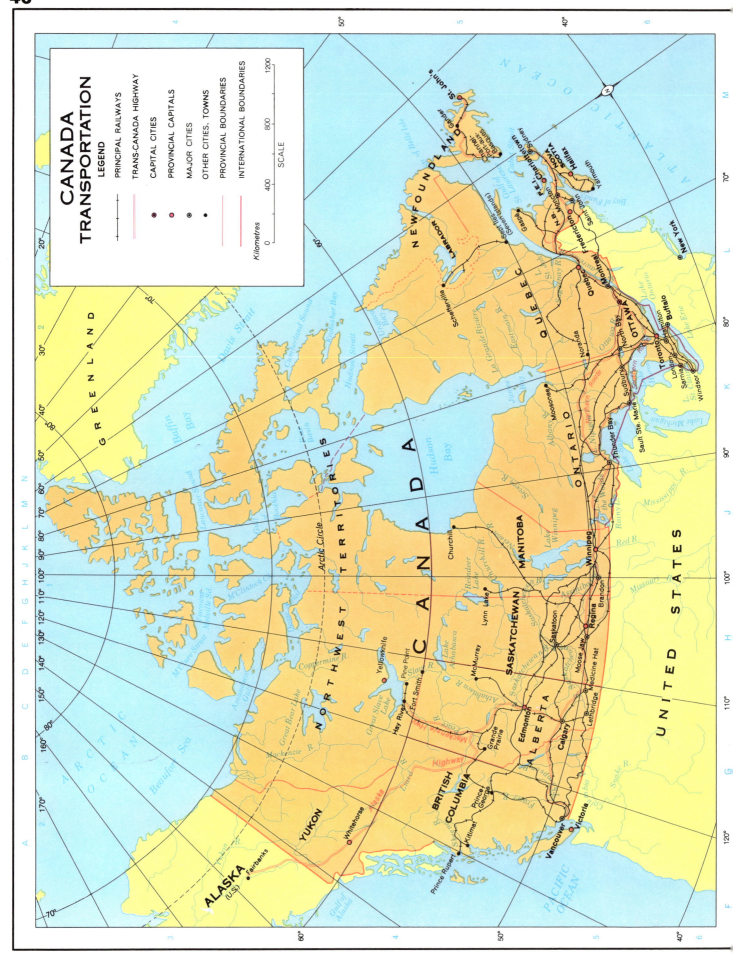

CANADA TRANSPORTATION

LEGEND

PRINCIPAL RAILWAYS

TRANS-CANADA HIGHWAY

CAPITAL CITIES

PROVINCIAL CAPITALS

MAJOR CITIES

OTHER CITIES, TOWNS

PROVINCIAL BOUNDARIES

INTERNATIONAL BOUNDARIES

SCALE

Kilometres

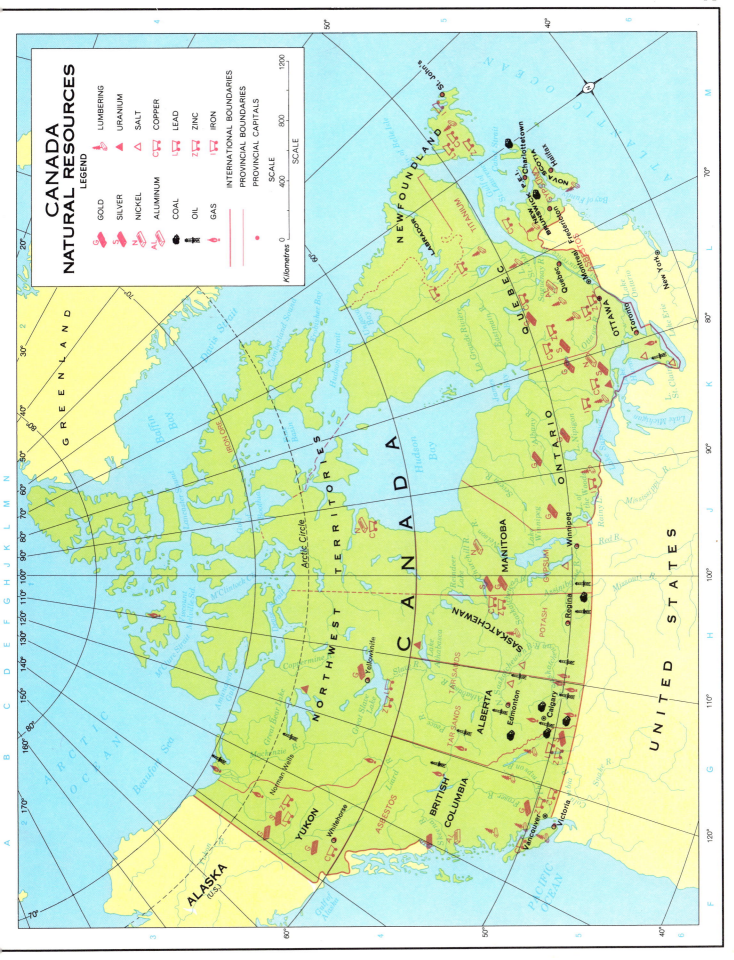

CANADA
NATURAL RESOURCES
LEGEND

G GOLD	LUMBERING	
S SILVER	URANIUM	SALT
N NICKEL	C COPPER	
AL ALUMINUM	L LEAD	
COAL	Z ZINC	
OIL	I IRON	
GAS		

INTERNATIONAL BOUNDARIES
PROVINCIAL BOUNDARIES
PROVINCIAL CAPITALS

SCALE
Kilometres 0   400   800   1200

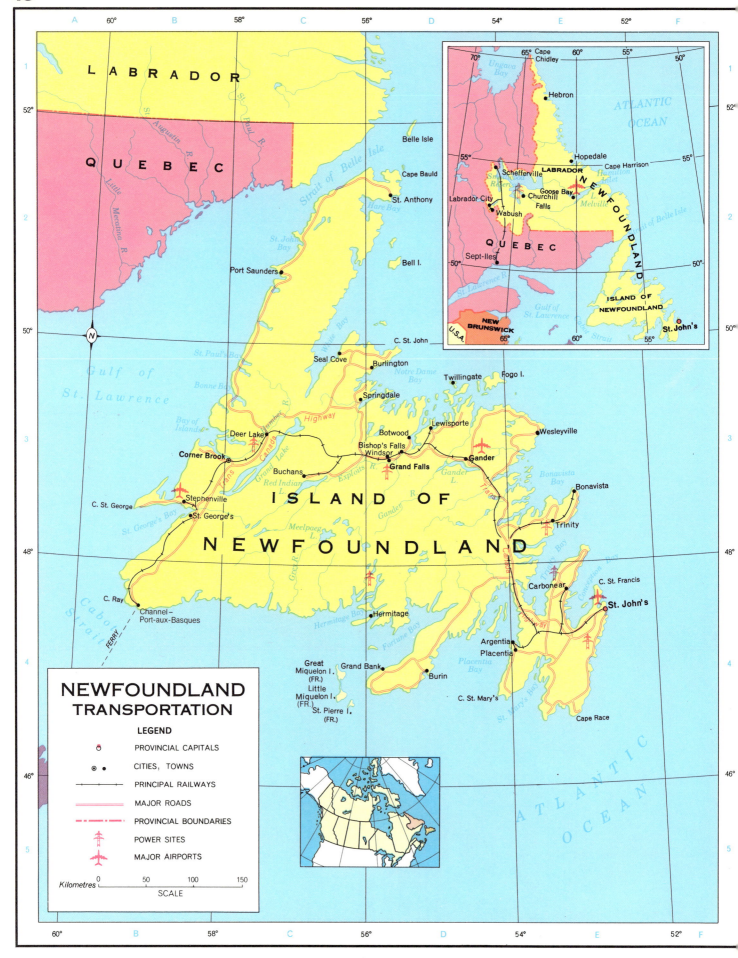

NEWFOUNDLAND
TRANSPORTATION

LEGEND

⚲	PROVINCIAL CAPITALS
⊙ ●	CITIES, TOWNS
┼┼┼	PRINCIPAL RAILWAYS
—	MAJOR ROADS
—·—·—	PROVINCIAL BOUNDARIES
⚡	POWER SITES
✈	MAJOR AIRPORTS

Kilometres 0   50   100   150

SCALE

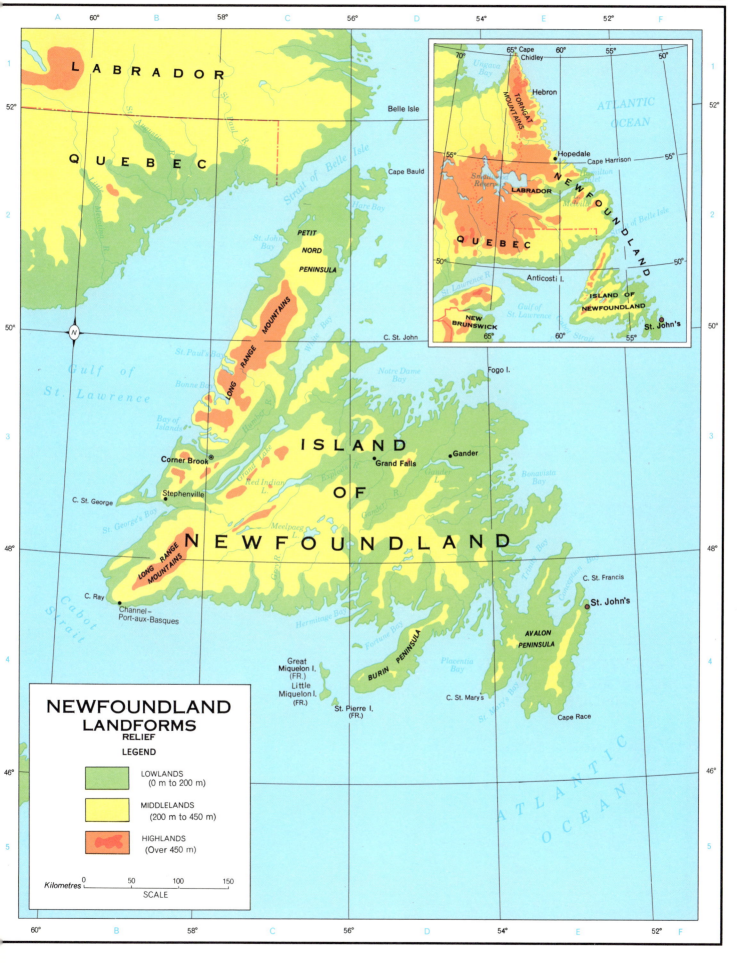

NEWFOUNDLAND LANDFORMS
RELIEF
LEGEND

LOWLANDS (0 m to 200 m)	
MIDDLELANDS (200 m to 450 m)	
HIGHLANDS (Over 450 m)	

Kilometres 0 50 100 150
SCALE

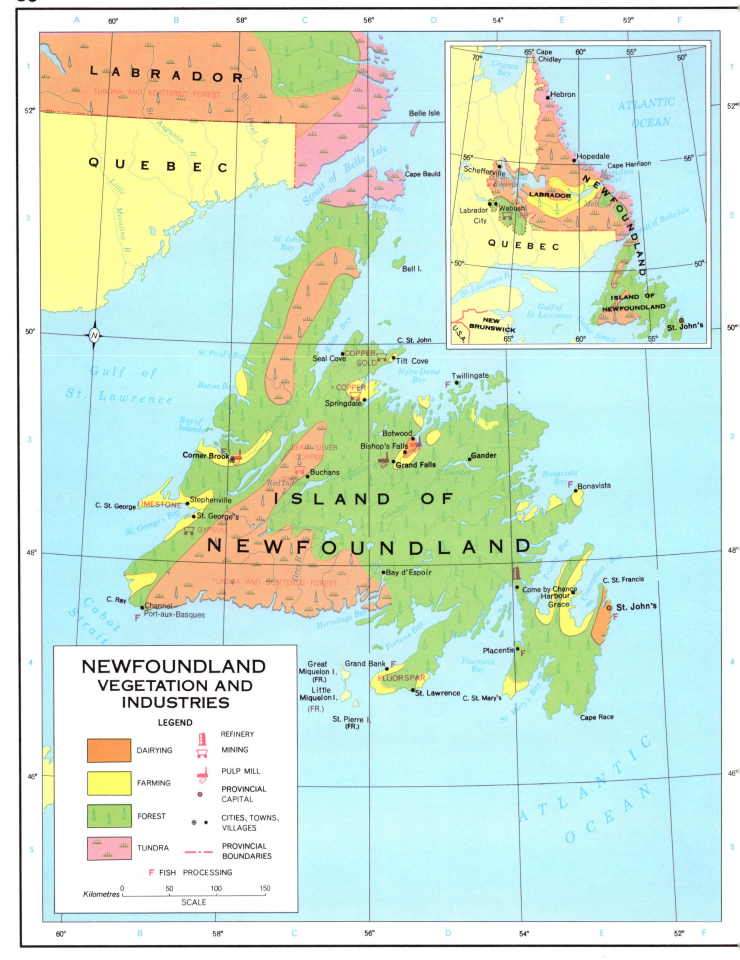

NEWFOUNDLAND VEGETATION AND INDUSTRIES

LEGEND

DAIRYING	REFINERY
FARMING	MINING
FOREST	PULP MILL
TUNDRA	PROVINCIAL CAPITAL
	CITIES, TOWNS, VILLAGES
	PROVINCIAL BOUNDARIES
F FISH PROCESSING	

Kilometres 0 50 100 150
SCALE

LABRADOR
TUNDRA AND SCATTERED FOREST
QUEBEC

Belle Isle
Cape Bauld
Strait of Belle Isle
Hare Bay
St. John Bay
Bell I.

Cape Chidley
Hebron
ATLANTIC OCEAN
Hopedale
Cape Harrison
Schefferville
LABRADOR
Labrador City
Wabush
QUEBEC
NEW BRUNSWICK
U.S.A.
St. Lawrence R.
Gulf of St. Lawrence
Cabot Strait
ISLAND OF NEWFOUNDLAND
St. John's

C. St. John
Seal Cove COPPER GOLD Tilt Cove
Notre Dame Bay
Twillingate F
COPPER
Springdale
Gulf of St. Lawrence
St. Paul's Inlet
Bonne Bay
Bay of Islands
Humber R.
LEAD SILVER COPPER
Corner Brook F
Red Indian L.
ZINC
Buchans
Botwood
Bishop's Falls
Grand Falls
Gander
Gander L.
Bonavista Bay
Bonavista F
C. St. George LIMESTONE
Stephenville
GYPSUM
St. George's
St. George's Bay
Meelpaeg L.
ISLAND OF NEWFOUNDLAND
TUNDRA AND SCATTERED FOREST
Gander R.
Bay d'Espoir
Come by Chance
Harbour Grace
C. St. Francis
St. John's F
C. Ray
Channel Port-aux-Basques F
Cabot Strait
Hermitage Bay
Fortune Bay
Great Miquelon I. (FR.)
Little Miquelon I. (FR.)
St. Pierre I. (FR.)
Grand Bank F
FLUORSPAR
St. Lawrence
C. St. Mary's
Placentia
Placentia Bay
Trinity Bay
Conception Bay
St. Mary's Bay
Cape Race
ATLANTIC OCEAN

A 60° B 58° C 56° D 54° E 52° F

70° 65° Cape 60° 55° 50°
55°
50°

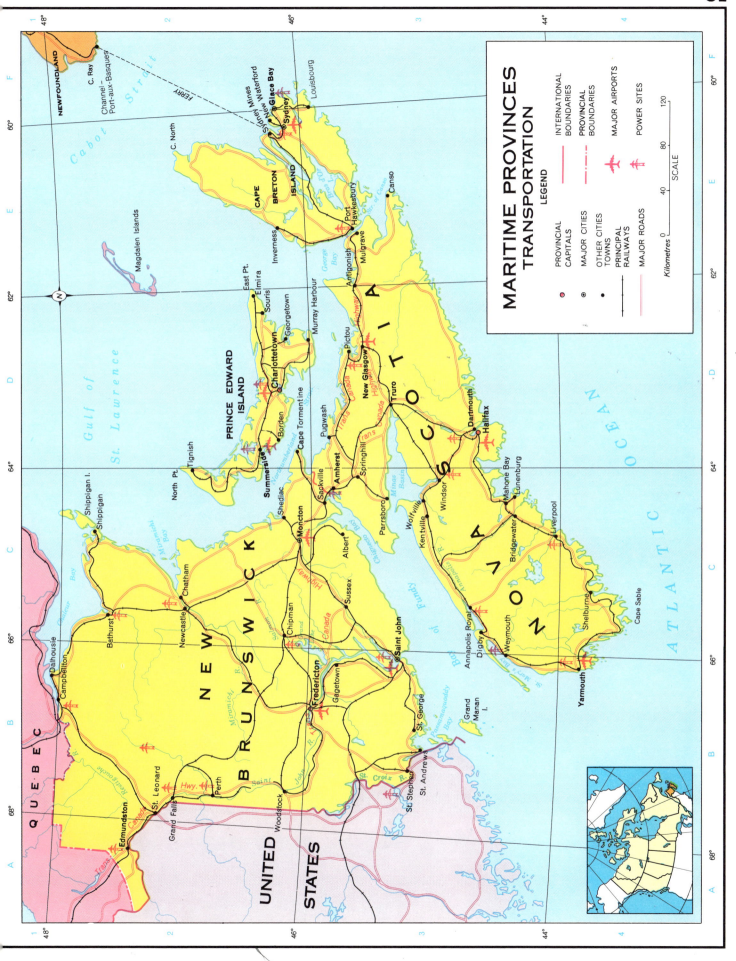

MARITIME PROVINCES
TRANSPORTATION

LEGEND

PROVINCIAL CAPITALS
MAJOR CITIES
OTHER CITIES TOWNS
PRINCIPAL RAILWAYS
MAJOR ROADS

INTERNATIONAL BOUNDARIES
PROVINCIAL BOUNDARIES
MAJOR AIRPORTS
POWER SITES

SCALE

Kilometres   0   40   80   120

NEWFOUNDLAND

C. Ray

Channel–Port-aux-Basques

FERRY

Cabot Strait

Magdalen Islands

Gulf of St. Lawrence

C. North

CAPE BRETON ISLAND

Sydney Mines
New Waterford
Glace Bay
Sydney
Louisbourg

Inverness

Bras d'Or L.

Port Hawkesbury

George Bay

Str. of Canso

Canso

Mulgrave
Antigonish

Pictou
New Glasgow

Trans Canada Highway

Truro

Dartmouth
Halifax

Windsor
Wolfville
Kentville

Mahone Bay
Lunenburg

Bridgewater
Liverpool

Shelburne

Cape Sable

ATLANTIC OCEAN

NOVA SCOTIA

Minas Basin

Parrsboro

Springhill
Amherst
Sackville

Pugwash

Cape Tormentine

Cumberland Basin

Chignecto Bay

Shediac
Moncton

Borden

Summerside

Tignish
North Pt.

PRINCE EDWARD ISLAND

East Pt.
Elmira
Souris
Georgetown
Murray Harbour

Charlottetown

Northumberland Strait

Shippigan I.
Shippigan

Miramichi Bay

Bathurst

Newcastle
Chatham

Miramichi R.

NEW BRUNSWICK

Albert

Chipman

Sussex

Saint John

Trans Canada Highway

Gagetown

Fredericton

St. George

St. Andrews

St. Stephen

St. Croix R.

Grand Manan I.

Passamaquoddy Bay

Bay of Fundy

Annapolis Royal
Digby
Weymouth

Yarmouth

Annapolis R.

R. Mersey

Campbellton
Dalhousie

QUEBEC

St. Leonard
Perth

Grand Falls
Edmundston

Woodstock

Trans Canada Hwy.

Restigouche R.

Saint John R.

Salmon R.

Chatham

UNITED STATES

52

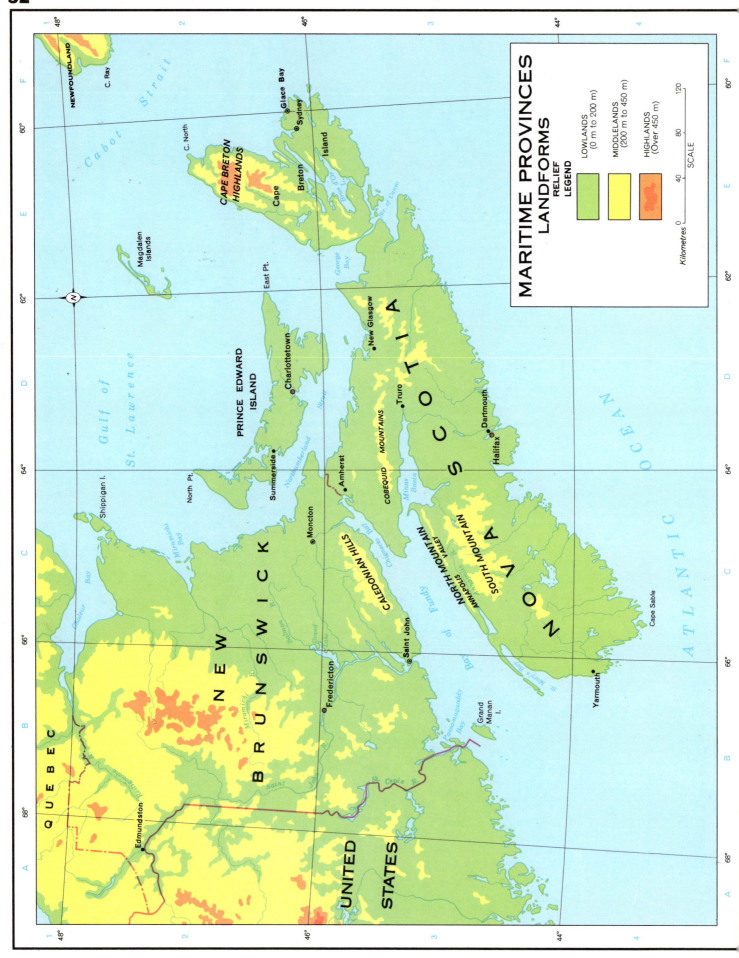

MARITIME PROVINCES
LANDFORMS
RELIEF
LEGEND

LOWLANDS
(0 m to 200 m)

MIDDLELANDS
(200 m to 450 m)

HIGHLANDS
(Over 450 m)

SCALE

Kilometres

0   40   80   120

NEWFOUNDLAND

C. Ray

Cabot Strait

Glace Bay
Sydney

C. North

CAPE BRETON HIGHLANDS

Cape Breton Island

Magdalen Islands

East Pt.

George Bay

New Glasgow

Bras d'Or L.

Str. of Canso

PRINCE EDWARD ISLAND

Charlottetown

Gulf of St. Lawrence

Truro

COBEQUID MOUNTAINS

Minas Basin

Dartmouth

Halifax

N O V A   S C O T I A

Shippigan I.

North Pt.

Summerside

Northumberland Str.

Moncton

Amherst

Chaleur Bay

Miramichi Bay

Grand Lake

Salmon R.

CALEDONIAN HILLS

Chignecto Bay

NORTH MOUNTAIN

ANNAPOLIS VALLEY

SOUTH MOUNTAIN

Cape Sable

N E W   B R U N S W I C K

Fundy

Saint John

Fredericton

Miramichi R.

Saint John R.

Bay

of

St. Mary's Bay

Yarmouth

Grand Manan I.

Passamaquoddy Bay

St. Croix R.

Q U E B E C

Restigouche R.

Edmundston

UNITED STATES

ATLANTIC OCEAN

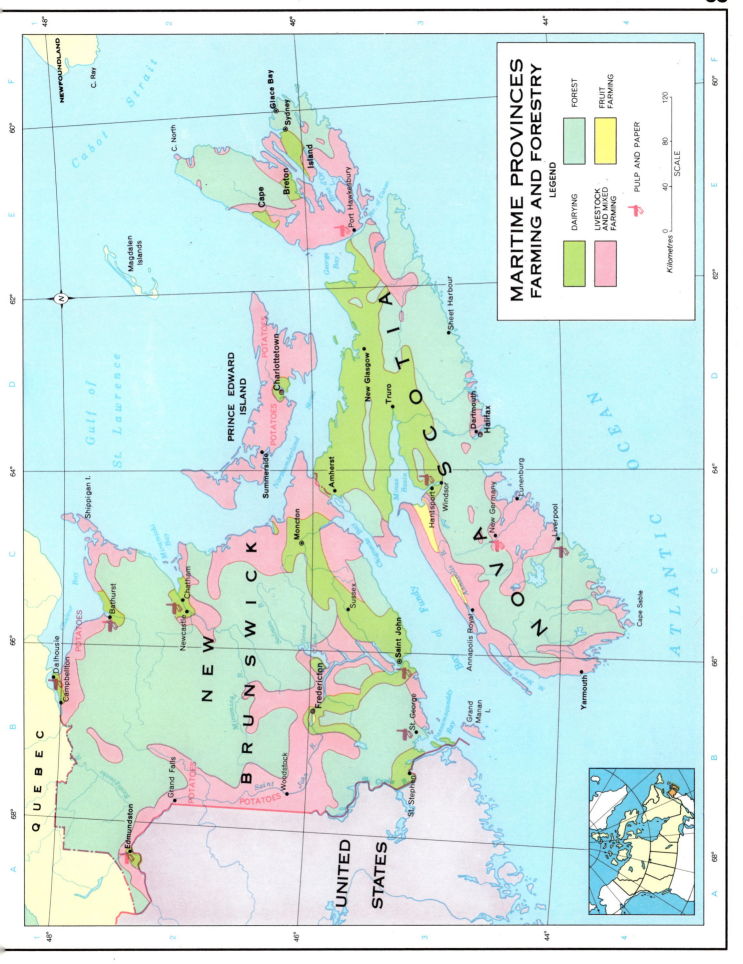

MARITIME PROVINCES
FARMING AND FORESTRY

LEGEND

DAIRYING

FOREST

LIVESTOCK
AND MIXED
FARMING

FRUIT
FARMING

PULP AND PAPER

PULP AND PAPER

Kilometres 0 40 80 120

SCALE

NEWFOUNDLAND

C. Ray

Cabot Strait

C. North

Glace Bay
Sydney

Cape Breton Island

Magdalen
Islands

George Bay

Port Hawkesbury

Gulf of St. Lawrence

PRINCE EDWARD ISLAND

POTATOES

Charlottetown

POTATOES

Summerside

Sheet Harbour

Amherst

New Glasgow

Truro

S C O T I A

Dartmouth
Halifax

Shippigan I.

Moncton

Hantsport
Windsor

Lunenburg

N O V A

New Germany

Liverpool

Bathurst

POTATOES

Chatham

Newcastle

Sussex

Bay of Fundy

Cape Sable

QUEBEC

Dalhousie
Campbellton

N E W

POTATOES

Fredericton

Saint John

St. George

Annapolis Royal

Yarmouth

B R U N S W I C K

St. Stephen

Grand Manan I.

A T L A N T I C   O C E A N

Grand Falls

POTATOES

Woodstock

Saint R.

POTATOES

Edmundston

UNITED STATES

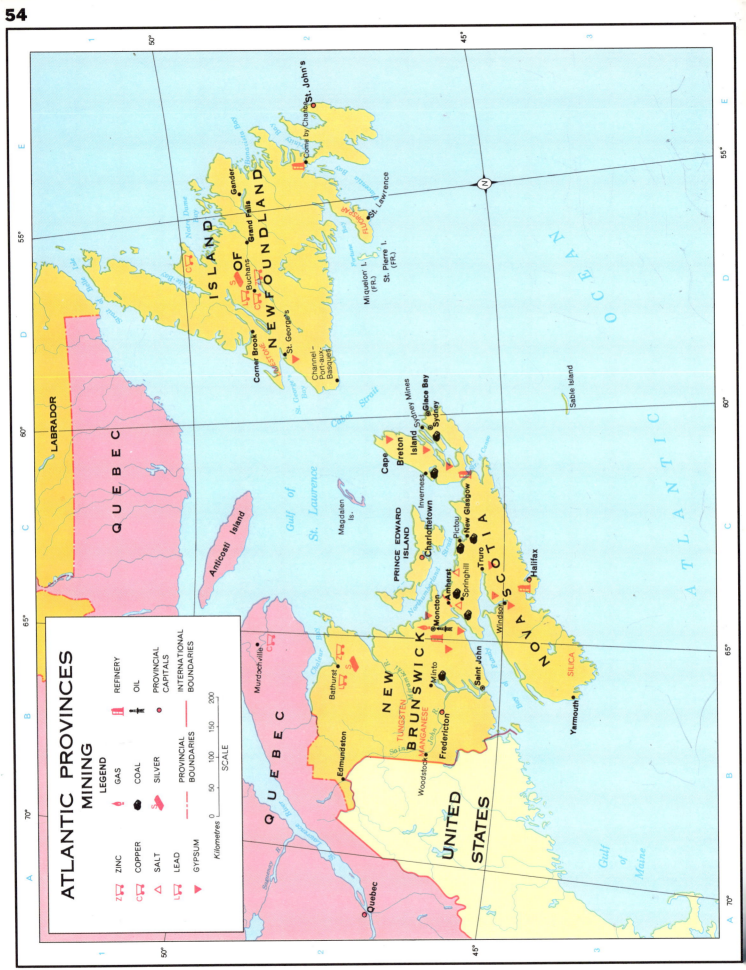

54

ATLANTIC PROVINCES
MINING
LEGEND

Z ZINC	**GAS**	**REFINERY**	**PROVINCIAL CAPITALS**
C COPPER	**COAL**	**OIL**	**INTERNATIONAL BOUNDARIES**
S SALT	**SILVER**		
L LEAD	**PROVINCIAL BOUNDARIES**		
GYPSUM			

SCALE
Kilometres
0 50 100 150 200

LABRADOR

QUEBEC

NEWFOUNDLAND

ISLAND OF

Come by Chance • St. John's

Gander

Grand Falls

Buchans

Corner Brook

St. George's

Channel-Port-aux-Basques

LIMESTONE

St. George's Bay

FLUORSPAR

St. Lawrence

Miquelon I. (FR.)

St. Pierre I. (FR.)

Fortune Bay

Bonavista Bay

Trinity Bay

Notre Dame Bay

White Bay

Strait of Belle Isle

Cabot Strait

Gulf of St. Lawrence

Anticosti Island

Magdalen Is.

Cape Breton

Island

Inverness

Sydney Mines

Glace Bay

Sydney

PRINCE EDWARD ISLAND

Charlottetown

Pictou

New Glasgow

Truro

NOVA SCOTIA

Halifax

Windsor

SILICA

Amherst

Springhill

Moncton

Minto

Saint John

Northumberland Strait

NEW BRUNSWICK

TUNGSTEN

MANGANESE

Bathurst

Murdochville

Edmundston

Woodstock

Fredericton

Saint John R.

Miramichi R.

Chaleur Bay

Bay of Fundy

QUEBEC

UNITED STATES

Quebec

St. Lawrence R.

Saguenay R.

Gulf of Maine

Sable Island

ATLANTIC OCEAN

N

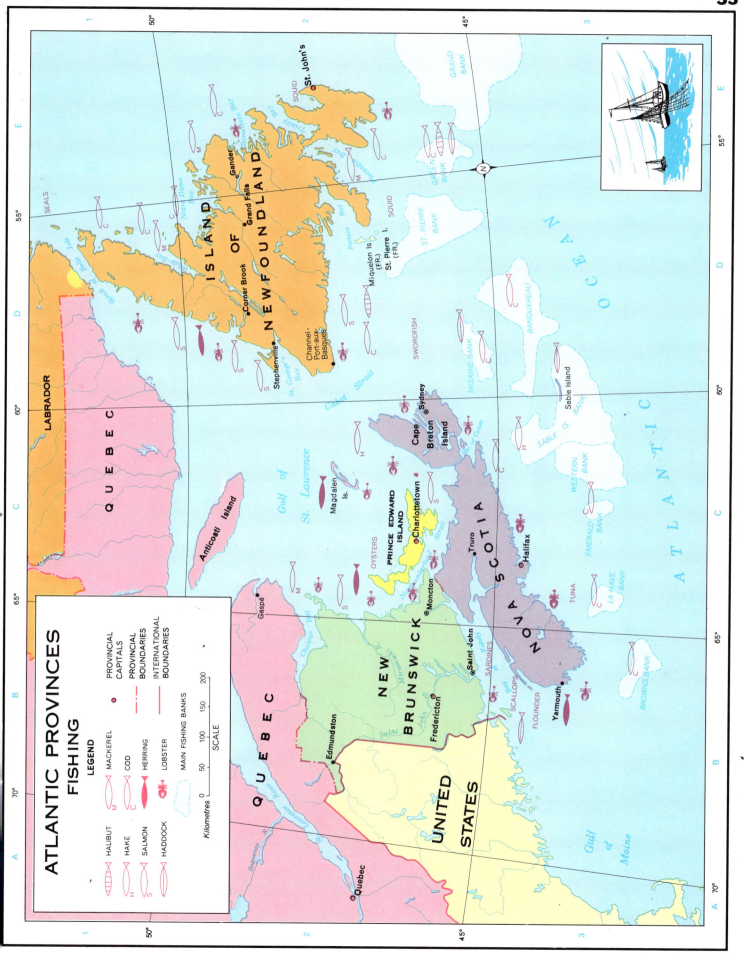

ATLANTIC PROVINCES
FISHING

LEGEND

●	PROVINCIAL CAPITALS
–·–·–	PROVINCIAL BOUNDARIES
——	INTERNATIONAL BOUNDARIES

MACKEREL
COD
HERRING
LOBSTER

HALIBUT
HAKE
SALMON
HADDOCK

MAIN FISHING BANKS

SCALE

Kilometres
0 50 100 150 200

LABRADOR

QUEBEC

ISLAND OF NEWFOUNDLAND

Gander
Grand Falls
Corner Brook
Stephenville
Channel-Port-aux-Basques
St. George's Bay

St. John's

SQUID

Bonavista Bay
Trinity Bay
Conception Bay
Placentia Bay
Fortune Bay

Notre Dame Bay
Strait of Belle Isle
White Bay

SEALS

Miquelon Is. (FR.)
St. Pierre I. (FR.)

SQUID

ST. PIERRE BANK

GREEN BANK

GRAND BANK

Cabot Strait

SWORDFISH

BANQUEREAU BANK

MISAINE BANK

Sable Island
SABLE IS. BANK

A T L A N T I C   O C E A N

QUEBEC

Anticosti Island

Gulf of St. Lawrence

Magdalen Is.

Gaspé

OYSTERS

PRINCE EDWARD ISLAND
Charlottetown

Cape Breton Island
Sydney

N O V A   S C O T I A
Truro
Halifax
Yarmouth

WESTERN BANK
EMERALD BANK
LA HAVE BANK

BROWNS BANK

NEW BRUNSWICK
Edmundston
Fredericton
Moncton
Saint John

SARDINES
SCALLOPS
FLOUNDER

TUNA

UNITED STATES

Gulf of Maine

Quebec

Saguenay R.
St. Lawrence River
Saint John R.
St. John R.
Miramichi R.

Chaleur Bay
Northumberland Strait
Cabot Strait

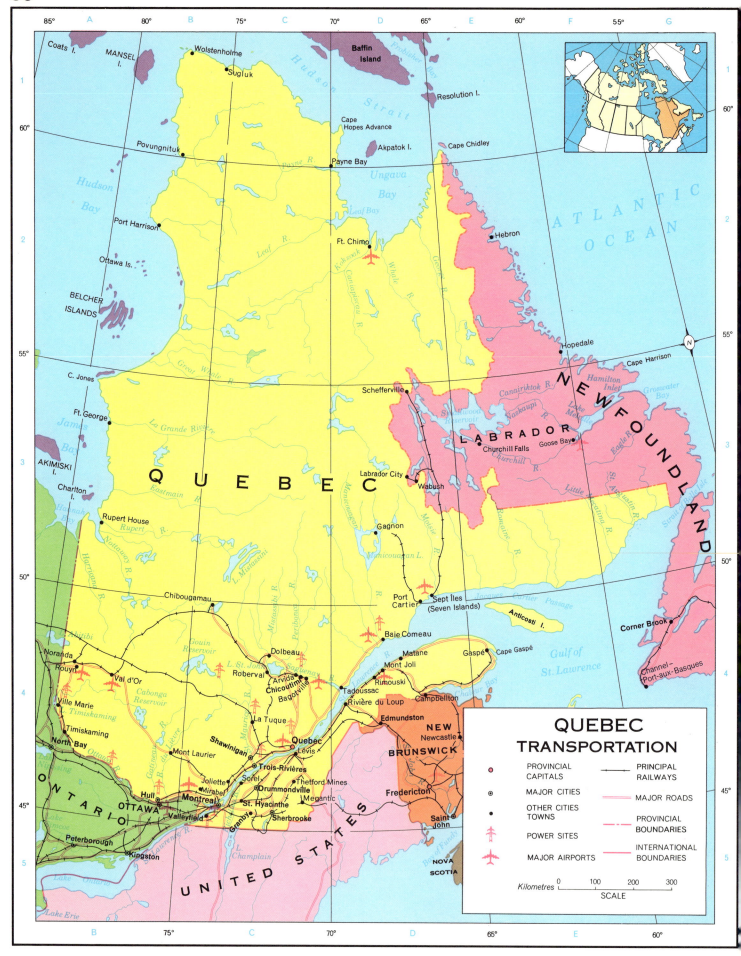

QUEBEC TRANSPORTATION

- ● PROVINCIAL CAPITALS
- ◎ MAJOR CITIES
- ● OTHER CITIES TOWNS
- ✈ POWER SITES
- ✈ MAJOR AIRPORTS

- ┼┼┼ PRINCIPAL RAILWAYS
- ══ MAJOR ROADS
- ─·─ PROVINCIAL BOUNDARIES
- ─── INTERNATIONAL BOUNDARIES

Kilometres 0   100   200   300
SCALE

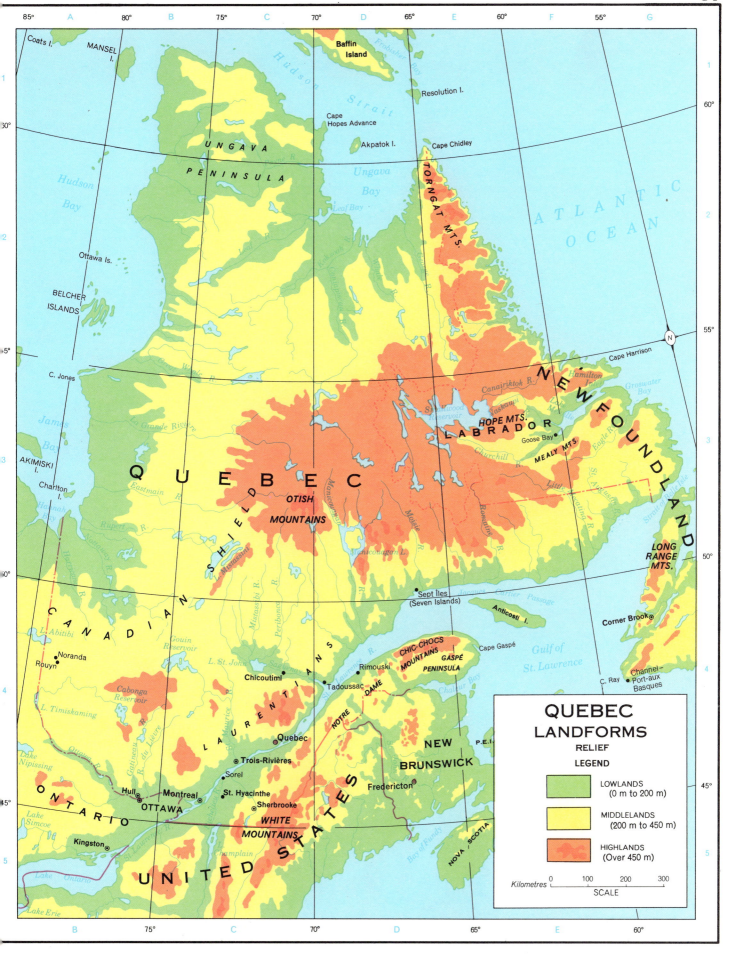

QUEBEC
LANDFORMS

RELIEF

LEGEND

LOWLANDS
(0 m to 200 m)

MIDDLELANDS
(200 m to 450 m)

HIGHLANDS
(Over 450 m)

Kilometres 0   100   200   300

SCALE

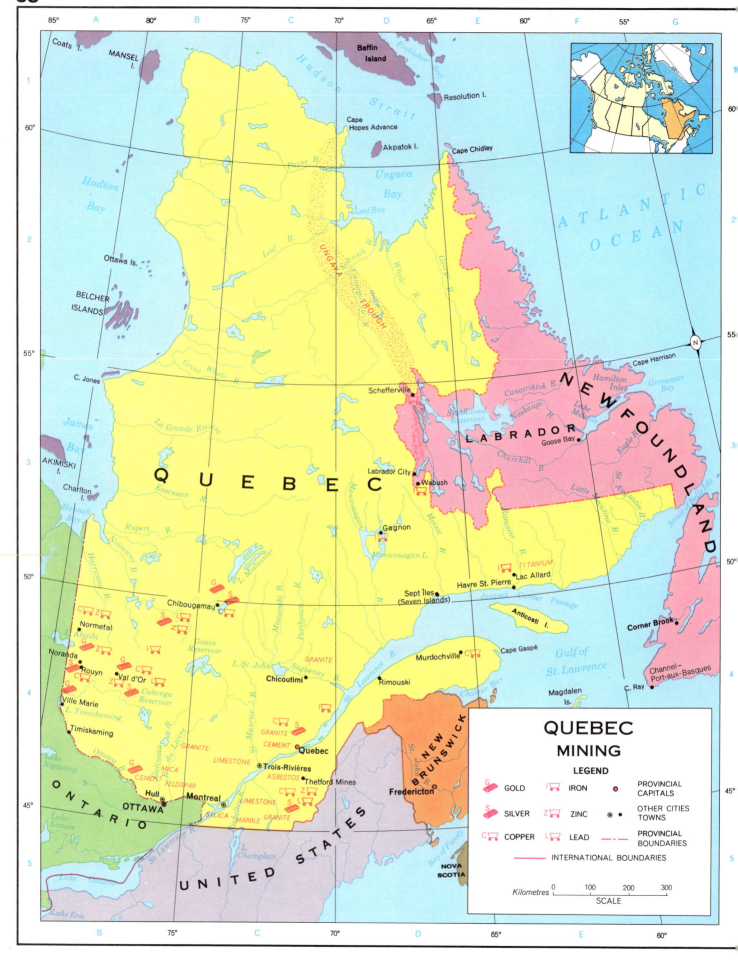

QUEBEC
MINING

LEGEND

G GOLD   I IRON   ⦿ PROVINCIAL CAPITALS

S SILVER   Z ZINC   ⦿ OTHER CITIES TOWNS

C COPPER   L LEAD   —·— PROVINCIAL BOUNDARIES

—— INTERNATIONAL BOUNDARIES

Kilometres 0 100 200 300
SCALE

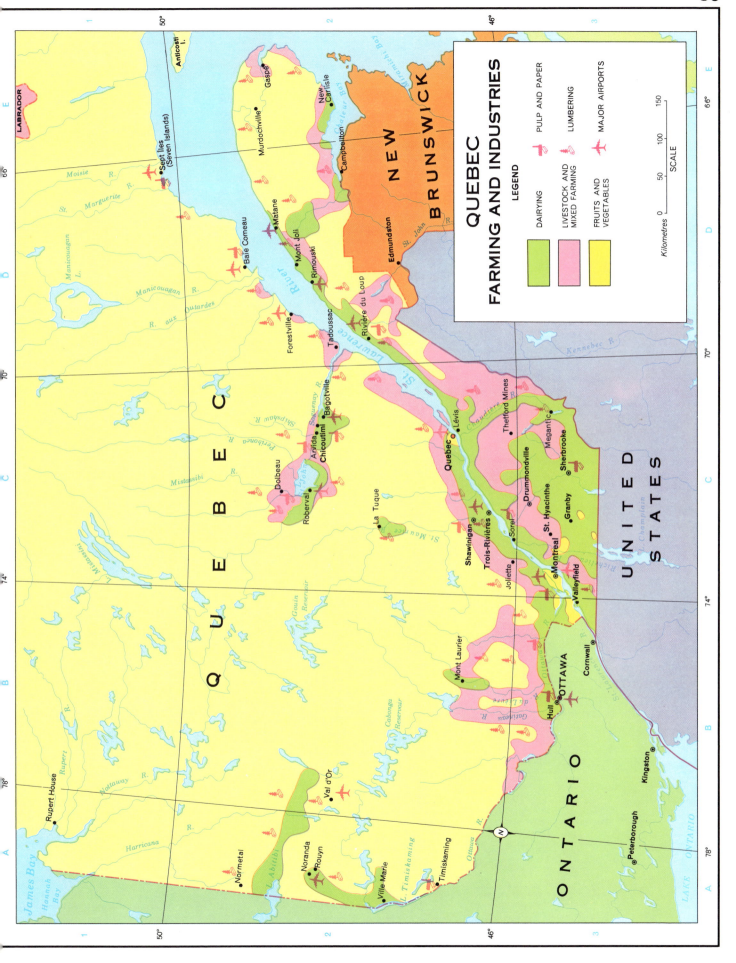

QUEBEC FARMING AND INDUSTRIES

LEGEND

DAIRYING

LIVESTOCK AND MIXED FARMING

FRUITS AND VEGETABLES

PULP AND PAPER

LUMBERING

MAJOR AIRPORTS

SCALE

Kilometres 0 50 100 150

LABRADOR

QUEBEC

ONTARIO

NEW BRUNSWICK

UNITED STATES

Anticosti I.

Gaspé

New Carlisle

Campbellton

Murdochville

Sept Iles (Seven Islands)

Matane

Baie Comeau

Mont Joli

Rimouski

Edmundston

Forestville

Tadoussac

Rivière du Loup

Arvida

Chicoutimi

Bagotville

Dolbeau

Roberval

La Tuque

Thetford Mines

Lévis

Quebec

Drummondville

Magantic

Sherbrooke

Shawinigan

Trois-Rivières

Sorel

St. Hyacinthe

Granby

Joliette

Montreal

Valleyfield

Mont Laurier

Hull

OTTAWA

Cornwall

Kingston

Peterborough

Rupert House

Val d'Or

Normetal

Noranda

Rouyn

Ville Marie

Timiskaming

Moisie R.

Manicouagan L.

Manicouagan R.

aux Outardes R.

St. Marguerite R.

Saguenay R.

Shipshaw R.

Péribonca R.

Mistassibi R.

L. Mistassini

St. Lawrence River

Chaudière R.

St. Maurice R.

Gatineau R.

Ottawa R.

Richelieu R.

Kennebec R.

L. Champlain

James Bay

Hannah Bay

Rupert R.

Nottaway R.

Harricana R.

L. Abitibi

Cabonga Reservoir

Gouin Reservoir

L. Timiskaming

LAKE ONTARIO

Chaleur Bay

Baie des Chaleurs

St. John R.

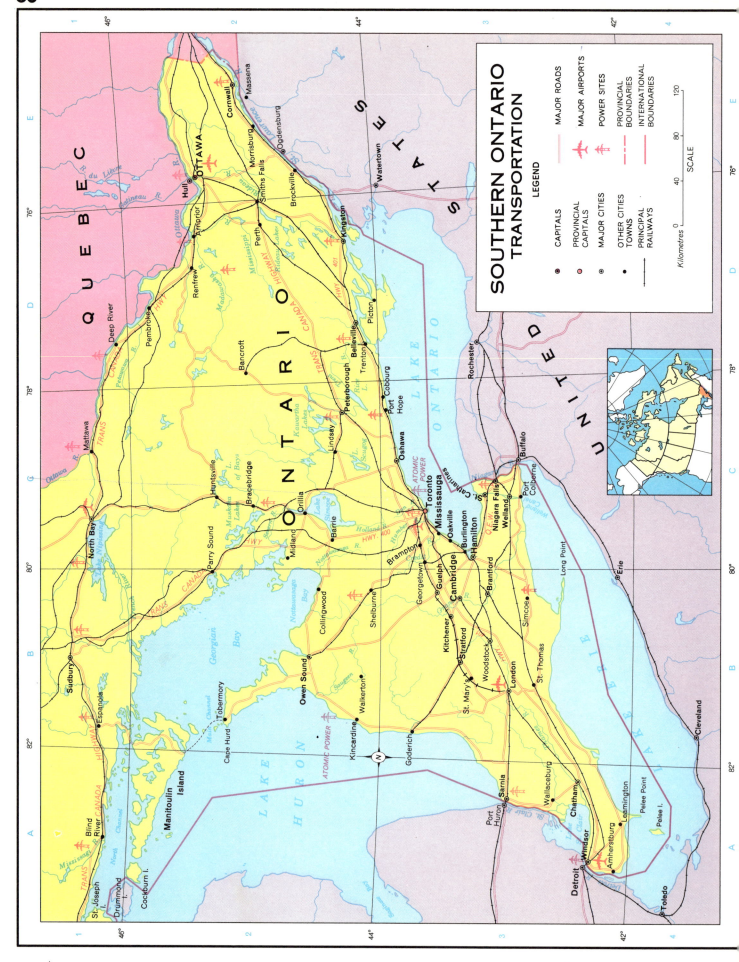

SOUTHERN ONTARIO TRANSPORTATION

LEGEND

MAJOR ROADS
MAJOR AIRPORTS
POWER SITES
PROVINCIAL BOUNDARIES
INTERNATIONAL BOUNDARIES

CAPITALS
PROVINCIAL CAPITALS
MAJOR CITIES
OTHER CITIES TOWNS
PRINCIPAL RAILWAYS

SCALE

0   40   80   120
Kilometres

QUEBEC

ONTARIO

UNITED STATES

LAKE ONTARIO

LAKE HURON

LAKE ERIE

Georgian Bay

Manitoulin Island

Ottawa
Hull
Cornwall
Massena
Ogdensburg
Morrisburg
Smiths Falls
Brockville
Arnprior
Renfrew
Perth
Watertown
Pembroke
Deep River
Bancroft
Kingston
Picton
Belleville
Trenton
Mattawa
Peterborough
Port Hope
Cobourg
Lindsay
Rochester
Huntsville
Bracebridge
Oshawa
ATOMIC POWER
North Bay
Orillia
Toronto
Mississauga
Buffalo
Parry Sound
Midland
Barrie
Brampton
Oakville
Burlington
Hamilton
St. Catharines
Niagara Falls
Welland
Port Colborne
Sudbury
Collingwood
Georgetown
Guelph
Cambridge
Brantford
Simcoe
Long Point
Erie
Espanola
Shelburne
Owen Sound
Kitchener
Stratford
Woodstock
London
St. Thomas
Cleveland
Blind River
Walkerton
St. Mary's
Tobermory
Cape Hurd
Kincardine
Goderich
Sarnia
Wallaceburg
Chatham
Leamington
Pelee Point
Pelee I.
St. Joseph I.
Drummond I.
Cockburn I.
Port Huron
Detroit
Windsor
Amherstburg
Toledo

TRANS CANADA HIGHWAY
HWY 401
HWY 400
ATOMIC POWER

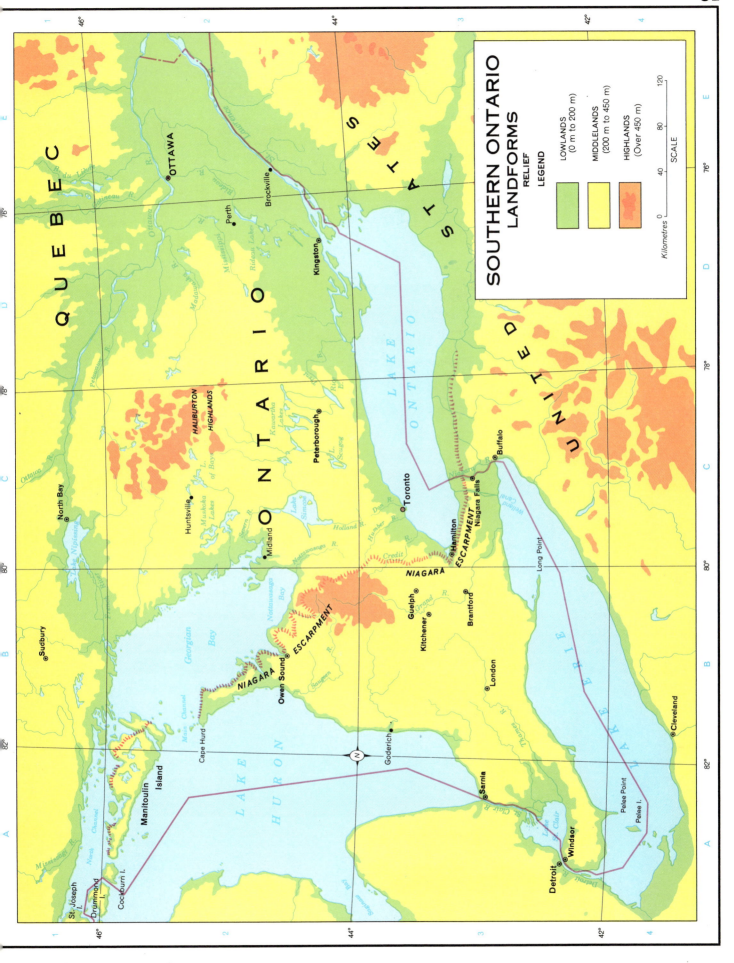

SOUTHERN ONTARIO
LANDFORMS
RELIEF
LEGEND

LOWLANDS
(0 m to 200 m)

MIDDLELANDS
(200 m to 450 m)

HIGHLANDS
(Over 450 m)

SCALE

Kilometres 0   40   80   120

QUEBEC

ONTARIO

UNITED STATES

OTTAWA

Brockville

Perth

Kingston

HALIBURTON
HIGHLANDS

Peterborough

North Bay

Huntsville

Muskoka Lakes

Lake Simcoe

Midland

Holland R.

Don R.

Humber R.

Toronto

LAKE ONTARIO

Buffalo

NIAGARA ESCARPMENT

Niagara Falls

Hamilton

NIAGARA

Credit R.

Welland Canal

Guelph

Grand R.

Brantford

Kitchener

London

Long Point

ESCARPMENT

Nottawasaga Bay

Nottawasaga R.

Owen Sound

NIAGARA

Georgian Bay

Sudbury

Lake Nipissing

Cape Hurd

Main Channel

Manitoulin Island

North Channel

Missisagi R.

St. Joseph I.

Drummond I.

Cockburn I.

LAKE HURON

Saugeen R.

Maitland R.

Goderich

Sarnia

St. Clair R.

Lake St. Clair

Detroit R.

Windsor

Detroit

Pelee Point

Pelee I.

Cleveland

LAKE ERIE

Thames R.

Ottawa R.

Rideau Lakes

Mississippi R.

Madawaska R.

Petawawa R.

R. du Lièvre

Gatineau R.

46°

44°

42°

76°

78°

80°

82°

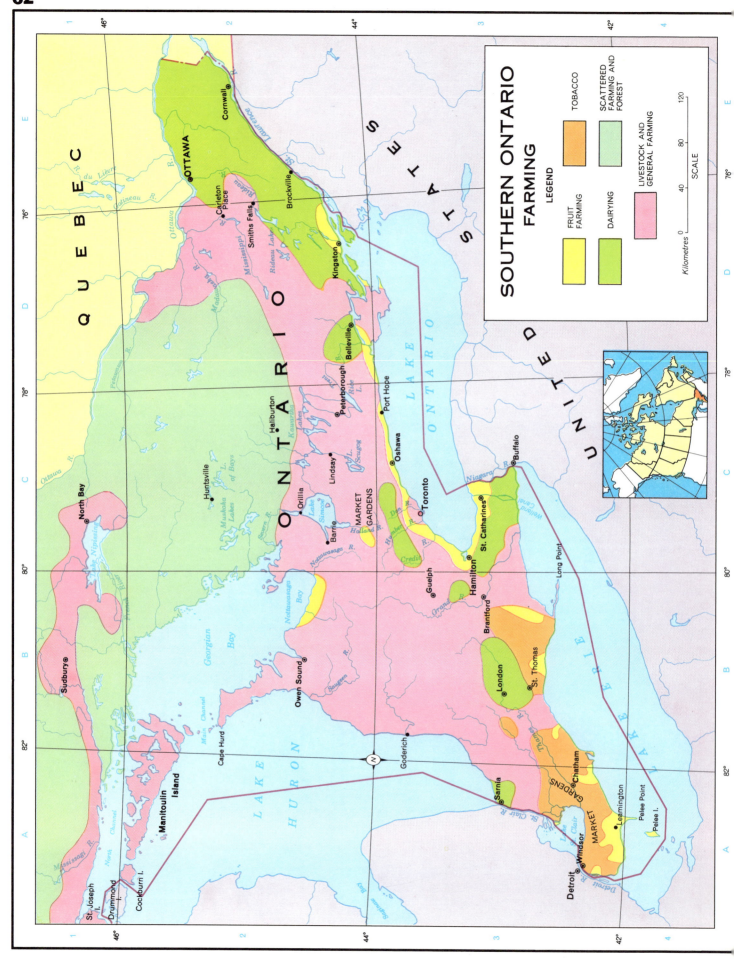

SOUTHERN ONTARIO
FARMING

LEGEND

- TOBACCO
- SCATTERED FARMING AND FOREST
- FRUIT FARMING
- DAIRYING
- LIVESTOCK AND GENERAL FARMING

SCALE

Kilometres   0   40   80   120

QUEBEC

ONTARIO

UNITED STATES

LAKE ONTARIO

LAKE ERIE

LAKE HURON

Georgian Bay

Manitoulin Island

Ottawa
Cornwall
Carleton Place
Smiths Falls
Brockville
Kingston
Belleville
Peterborough
Port Hope
Oshawa
Toronto
Buffalo
St. Catharines
Hamilton
Brantford
London
St. Thomas
Guelph
Long Point
Pelee Point
Pelee I.
Leamington
Chatham
MARKET GARDENS
Windsor
Detroit
Sarnia
Goderich
Owen Sound
Cape Hurd
North Bay
Sudbury
Huntsville
Haliburton
Lindsay
Orillia
Barrie
MARKET GARDENS
St. Joseph I.
Drummond I.
Cockburn I.

Lake Simcoe
Lake Nipissing
Muskoka Lakes
Lake of Bays
Rideau Lakes
Kawartha Lakes

Ottawa R.
Rideau R.
Mississippi R.
Madawaska R.
Petawawa R.
Gatineau R.
du Lièvre R.
St. Lawrence R.
Trent R.
Moira R.
Don R.
Humber R.
Credit R.
Grand R.
Thames R.
St. Clair R.
Detroit R.
Niagara R.
Welland Canal
Saugeen R.
Maitland R.
Nottawasaga R.
Severn R.
Mississagi R.
North Channel
Main Channel

Lake St. Clair

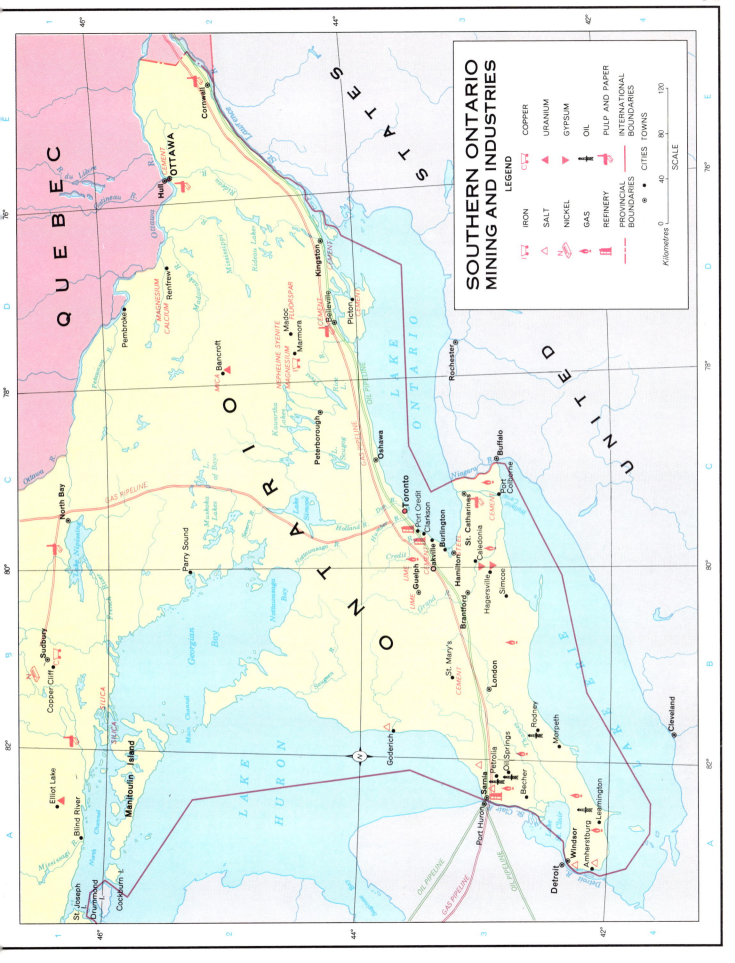

SOUTHERN ONTARIO MINING AND INDUSTRIES

Legend

COPPER	URANIUM	GYPSUM	OIL	PULP AND PAPER
IRON	SALT	NICKEL	GAS	REFINERY

INTERNATIONAL BOUNDARIES
PROVINCIAL BOUNDARIES
CITIES   TOWNS

SCALE
Kilometres 0   40   80   120

QUEBEC

ONTARIO

UNITED STATES

Cornwall
OTTAWA
Hull   CEMENT
R. du Lièvre
Gatineau R.
Ottawa R.
Mississippi R.
Rideau R.
Rideau Lakes
Kingston   CEMENT
Belleville   CEMENT
Picton   CEMENT
Pembroke
Renfrew   MAGNESIUM   CALCIUM
Madawaska R.
Petawawa R.
MICA Bancroft
NEPHELINE SYENITE   Madoc   FLUORSPAR
MAGNESIUM   Marmora
Trent R.
Kawartha Lakes
Rice L.
Scugog L.
Peterborough
North Bay
Lake Nipissing
Parry Sound
Muskoka Lakes
L. of Bays
Lake Simcoe
Holland R.
Nottawasaga R.
Severn R.
Don R.
Humber R.
Oshawa
Toronto
Port Credit
Clarkson
Burlington
Oakville   CEMENT
Guelph   LIME
Credit R.
LIME
Hamilton   STEEL
Brantford
Caledonia
Hagersville
Simcoe
St. Catharines   CEMENT
Welland Canal
Port Colborne
Buffalo
Rochester
Niagara R.
Sudbury
Copper Cliff
Elliot Lake
Blind River
Manitoulin Island
SILICA
St. Joseph I.
Drummond I.
Cockburn I.
Mississagi R.
North Channel
Main Channel
Georgian Bay
Nottawasaga Bay
Saugeen R.
Goderich
SILICA
St. Mary's   CEMENT
London
Grand R.
Rodney
Morpeth
Petrolia
Oil Springs
Becher
Sarnia
Port Huron
St. Clair R.
Thames R.
Leamington
Windsor
Amherstburg
Detroit
Detroit R.
Cleveland
GAS PIPELINE
OIL PIPELINE
OIL PIPELINE
GAS PIPELINE

LAKE ONTARIO
LAKE ERIE
LAKE HURON
St. Lawrence R.
Ottawa R.

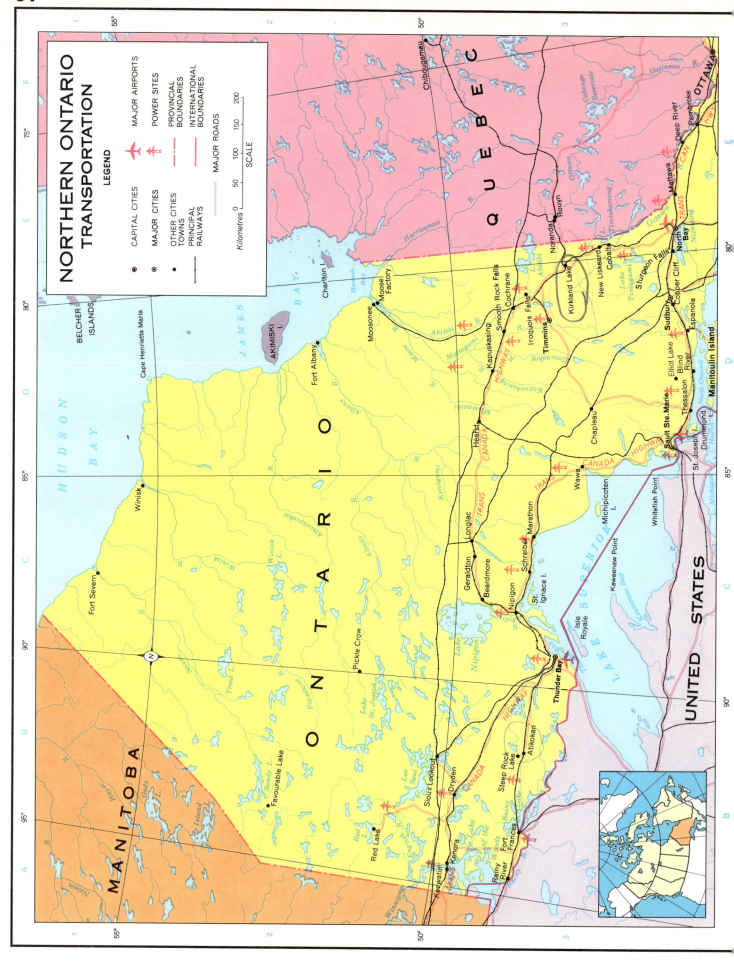

NORTHERN ONTARIO TRANSPORTATION

LEGEND

MAJOR AIRPORTS	
POWER SITES	
CAPITAL CITIES	PROVINCIAL BOUNDARIES
MAJOR CITIES	INTERNATIONAL BOUNDARIES
OTHER CITIES TOWNS	
PRINCIPAL RAILWAYS	MAJOR ROADS

SCALE

Kilometres 0   50   100   150   200

QUEBEC

ONTARIO

MANITOBA

UNITED STATES

HUDSON BAY

JAMES BAY

LAKE SUPERIOR

BELCHER ISLANDS

AKIMISKI I.

Cape Henrietta Maria

Charlton I.

Chibougamau

Ottawa

Pembroke
Deep River
Mattawa
North Bay
Rouyn
Noranda
Cobalt
New Liskeard
Sturgeon Falls
Kirkland Lake
Cochrane
Smooth Rock Falls
Kapuskasing
Iroquois Falls
Timmins
Moose Factory
Moosonee
Fort Albany
Sudbury
Copper Cliff
Espanola
Elliot Lake
Blind River
Thessalon
Sault Ste. Marie
St. Joseph I.
Drummond
Manitoulin Island
Chapleau
Hearst
Wawa
Michipicoten I.
Whitefish Point
Keweenaw Point
Isle Royale
Winisk
Fort Severn
Longlac
Geraldton
Beardmore
Nipigon
St. Ignace I.
Schreiber
Marathon
Nipigon
Thunder Bay
Pickle Crow
Sioux Lookout
Dryden
Atikokan
Steep Rock Lake
Red Lake
Keewatin
Kenora
Fort Frances
Rainy River
Favourable Lake

TRANS CANADA HIGHWAY

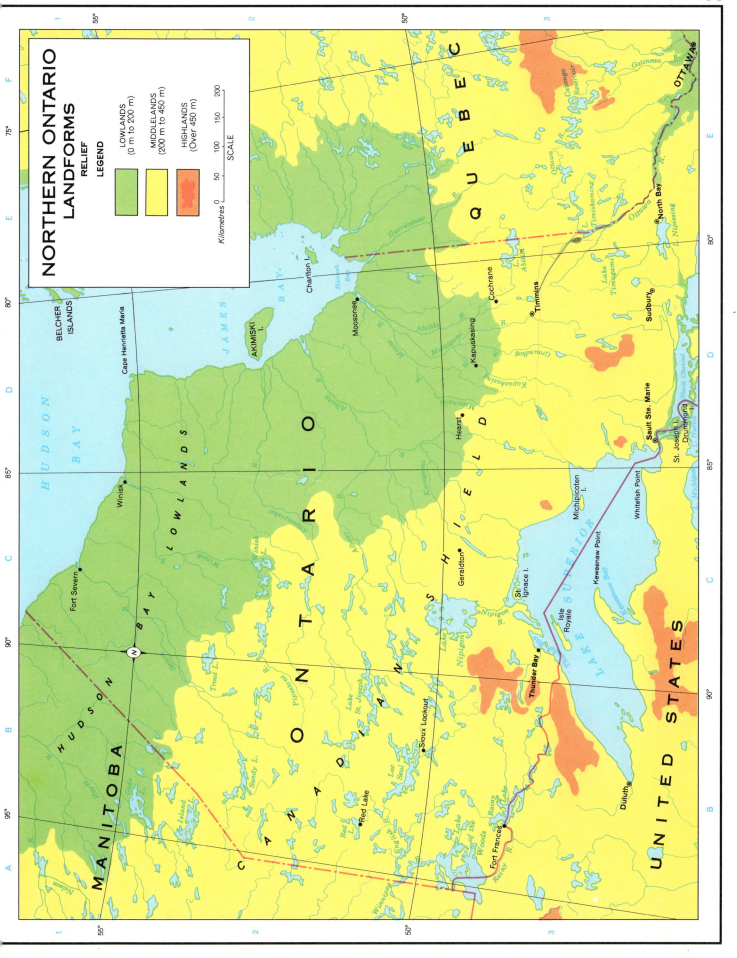

NORTHERN ONTARIO LANDFORMS

RELIEF

LEGEND

LOWLANDS
(0 m to 200 m)

MIDDLELANDS
(200 m to 450 m)

HIGHLANDS
(Over 450 m)

SCALE

Kilometres
0 50 100 150 200

QUEBEC

ONTARIO

MANITOBA

UNITED STATES

HUDSON BAY

JAMES BAY

LAKE SUPERIOR

HUDSON BAY LOWLANDS

CANADIAN SHIELD

BELCHER ISLANDS

Cape Henrietta Maria

Charlton I.

Hannah Bay

AKIMISKI I.

Moosonee

Ottawa

OTTAWA

Gatineau R.

Cabonga Reservoir

L. Timiskaming

Cochrane

Timmins

Kapuskasing

Sudbury

North Bay

L. Nipissing

Lake Timagami

L. Abitibi

Groundhog R.

Abitibi R.

Moose R.

Mattagami R.

Kapuskasing R.

Missinaibi R.

Hearst

Albany R.

Kenogami R.

Sault Ste. Marie

St. Joseph I.

Drummond I.

Michipicoten

Whitefish Point

Keweenaw Point

Keweenaw Bay

Michipicoten R.

Geraldton

St. Ignace I.

Isle Royale

Nipigon R.

Lake Nipigon

Thunder Bay

Duluth

Winisk

Winisk R.

Attawapiskat R.

Ekwan R.

Fort Severn

Severn R.

Trout L.

Pipestone R.

Sioux Lookout

Lake St. Joseph

Sandy L.

Island L.

Gods R.

Hayes R.

Nelson R.

Red Lake

Red L.

Lac Seul

English R.

Lake of the Woods

Fort Frances

Rainy R.

Rainy L.

Winnipeg R.

Harricanaw R.

Moose R.

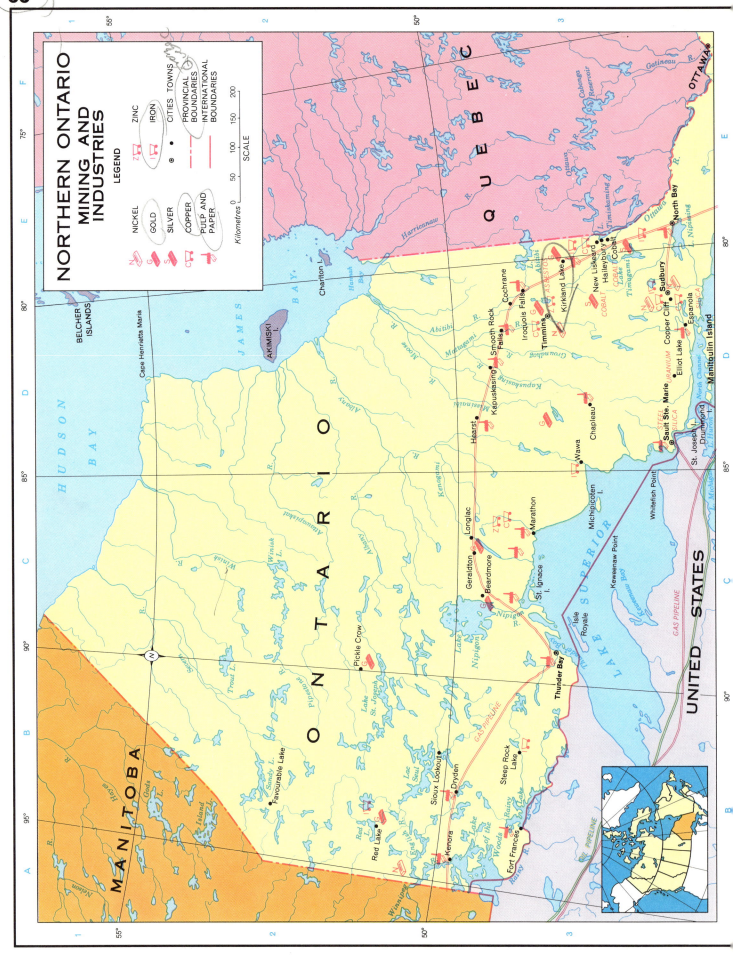

NORTHERN ONTARIO MINING AND INDUSTRIES

LEGEND

ZINC Z
IRON I

NICKEL N
GOLD G
SILVER S
COPPER C
PULP AND PAPER

CITIES TOWNS ●
⊙

PROVINCIAL BOUNDARIES
INTERNATIONAL BOUNDARIES

SCALE

Kilometres 0 50 100 150 200

QUEBEC

MANITOBA

ONTARIO

UNITED STATES

HUDSON BAY

JAMES BAY

LAKE SUPERIOR

Belcher Islands
Cape Henrietta Maria
Akimiski I.
Charlton I.
Hannah Bay

Ottawa
North Bay
New Liskeard
Haileybury
Cobalt
Timagami
Sudbury
Copper Cliff
Espanola
Elliot Lake
Manitoulin Island
Cochrane
Iroquois Falls
Smooth Rock Falls
Kapuskasing
Hearst
Kirkland Lake
Timmins
Chapleau
Wawa
Sault Ste. Marie
St. Joseph I.
Drummond
Whitefish Point
Michipicoten I.
Isle Royale
Keweenaw Point
Keweenaw Bay
Longlac
Geraldton
Beardmore
Marathon
St. Ignace I.
Thunder Bay
Pickle Crow
Sioux Lookout
Dryden
Kenora
Fort Frances
Steep Rock Lake
Red Lake
Favourable Lake
Sandy L.

COBALT
ASBESTOS
URANIUM
STEEL
SILICA
GAS PIPELINE

Abitibi R.
Mattagami R.
Groundhog R.
Kapuskasing R.
Missinaibi R.
Albany R.
Kenogami R.
Moose R.
Winisk R.
Attawapiskat R.
Severn R.
Winnipeg R.
Nelson R.
Hayes R.
God's L.
Island L.
Trout L.
Pipestone R.
Lake St. Joseph
Lac Seul
Lake of the Woods
Rainy Lake
Rainy R.
English R.
Lake Nipigon
Nipigon R.
Lake Timiskaming
Lake Abitibi
Harricanaw R.
Ottawa R.
Gatineau R.
Cabonga Reservoir
L. Nipissing
North Channel
Lake Huron
L. Michigan

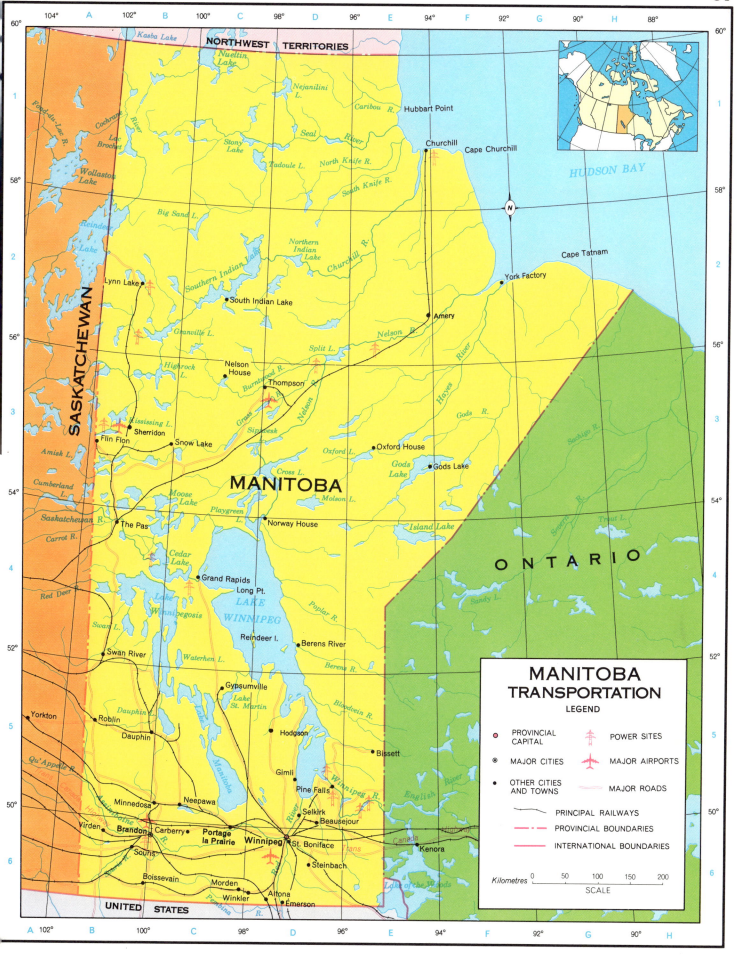

MANITOBA
TRANSPORTATION
LEGEND

PROVINCIAL CAPITAL
MAJOR CITIES
OTHER CITIES AND TOWNS
POWER SITES
MAJOR AIRPORTS
MAJOR ROADS
PRINCIPAL RAILWAYS
PROVINCIAL BOUNDARIES
INTERNATIONAL BOUNDARIES

Kilometres 0   50   100   150   200
SCALE

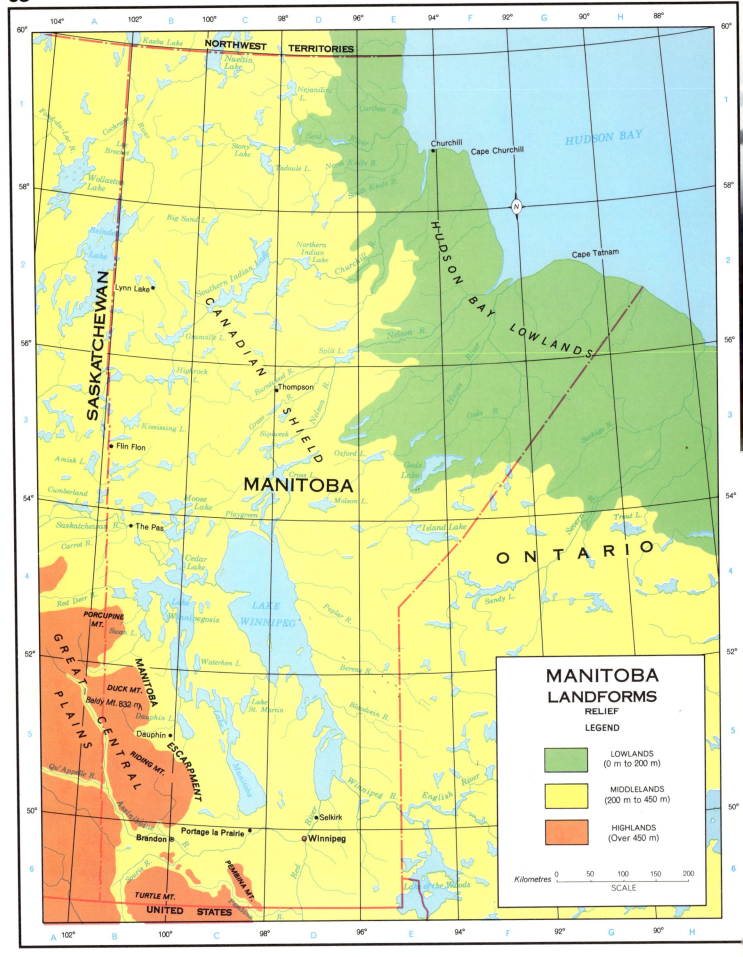

MANITOBA
LANDFORMS
RELIEF
LEGEND

🟩	LOWLANDS (0 m to 200 m)
🟨	MIDDLELANDS (200 m to 450 m)
🟧	HIGHLANDS (Over 450 m)

Kilometres 0 50 100 150 200
SCALE

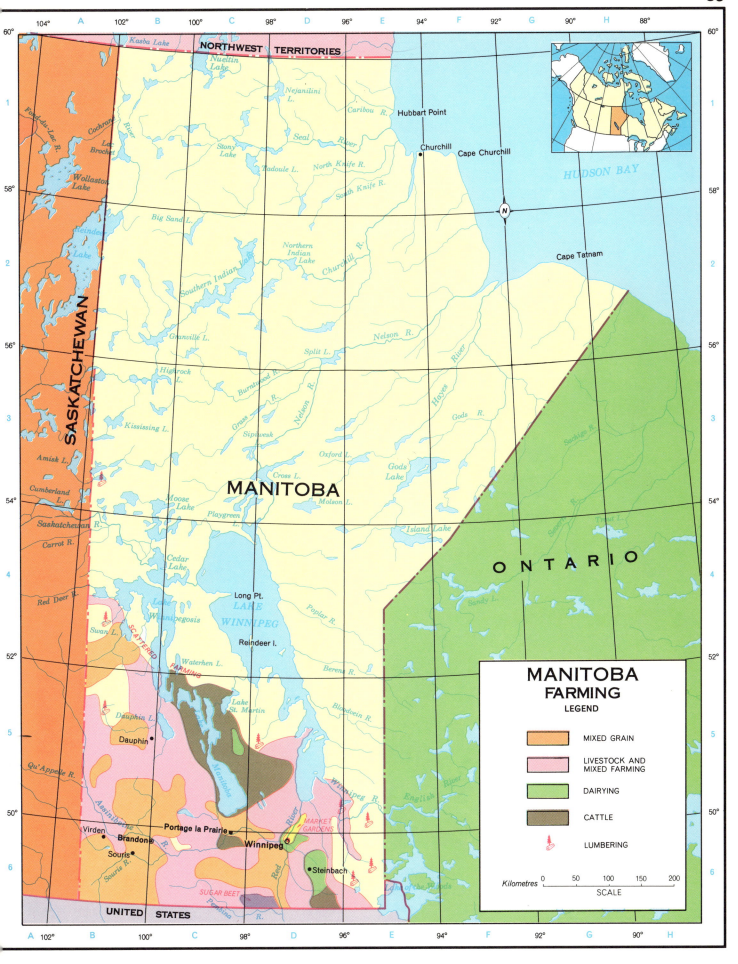

MANITOBA
FARMING
LEGEND

▨	MIXED GRAIN
▨	LIVESTOCK AND MIXED FARMING
▨	DAIRYING
▨	CATTLE
🌲	LUMBERING

Kilometres 0   50   100   150   200
SCALE

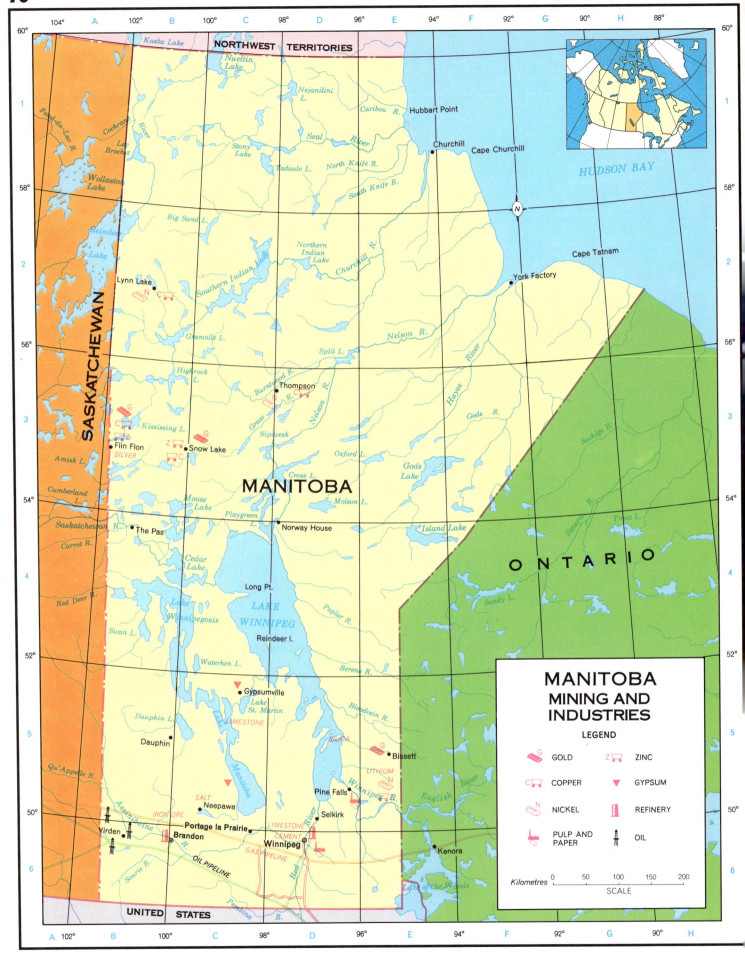

NORTHWEST TERRITORIES

Kasba Lake

Nueltin Lake

HUDSON BAY

Hubbart Point

Churchill
Cape Churchill

Cape Tatnam

York Factory

SASKATCHEWAN

Ford-du-Lac R.

Cochrane River

Lac Brochet

Wollaston Lake

Reindeer Lake

Amisk L.

Cumberland L.

Saskatchewan R.

Carrot R.

Red Deer R.

Qu'Appelle R.

Big Sand L.

Stony Lake

Tadoule L.

Seal River

North Knife R.

South Knife R.

Caribou R.

Nejanilini L.

Northern Indian Lake

Southern Indian Lake

Granville L.

Highrock L.

Churchill R.

Split L.

Nelson R.

Nelson River

Hayes River

Gods R.

Sachigo R.

Lynn Lake N C

Kississing L.

G

C Z
Flin Flon Z
SILVER C
Snow Lake

G

Burntwood R. C
Thompson

Grass R.

Sipiwesk L.

Oxford L.

Gods Lake

Island Lake

Severn R.

Trout L.

MANITOBA

Moose Lake

The Pas

Cedar Lake

Playgreen L.

Norway House

Cross L.

Molson L.

ONTARIO

Sandy L.

Lake Winnipegosis

Long Pt.

LAKE WINNIPEG

Reindeer I.

Swan L.

Waterhen L.

Berens R.

Poplar R.

Bloodvein R.

Sachigo R.

Dauphin L.

Gypsumville

Lake St. Martin

LIMESTONE

SILICA

G
Bissett

English River

Dauphin

LITHIUM
N

Manitoba River

Pine Falls

Winnipeg R.

SALT

Neepawa

IRON ORE

Virden

Portage la Prairie
Brandon

Selkirk

Winnipeg
LIMESTONE
CEMENT

Kenora

Assiniboine R.

OIL PIPELINE

Souris R.

GAS PIPELINE

Red River

Lake of the Woods

Pembina R.

UNITED STATES

N

**MANITOBA
MINING AND
INDUSTRIES**

LEGEND

G **GOLD**   Z **ZINC**

C **COPPER**   ▼ **GYPSUM**

N **NICKEL**   **REFINERY**

**PULP AND
PAPER**   **OIL**

Kilometres 0   50   100   150   200
SCALE

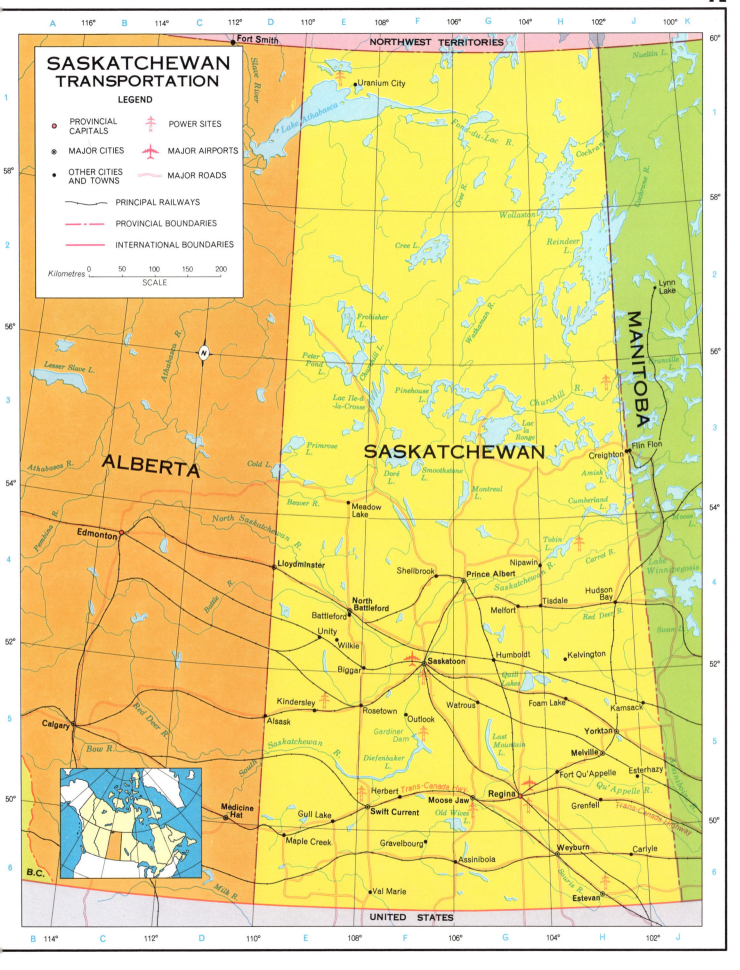

SASKATCHEWAN
TRANSPORTATION
LEGEND

- ● PROVINCIAL CAPITALS
- ◉ MAJOR CITIES
- ● OTHER CITIES AND TOWNS
- ⟟ POWER SITES
- ✈ MAJOR AIRPORTS
- ≈ MAJOR ROADS
- ～ PRINCIPAL RAILWAYS
- ·—·—· PROVINCIAL BOUNDARIES
- —— INTERNATIONAL BOUNDARIES

Kilometres
SCALE
0 50 100 150 200

NORTHWEST TERRITORIES

Fort Smith
Slave River
Uranium City
Lake Athabasca
Fond-du-Lac R.
Nueltin L.
Cochrane R.
Cree R.
Wollaston L.
Cree L.
Reindeer L.
Lynn Lake
Granville L.

MANITOBA

Frobisher L.
Washaman R.
Peter Pond L.
Churchill L.
Pinehouse L.
Churchill R.
Lac Ile-à-la-Crosse
Lac la Ronge
Amisk L.
Flin Flon
Creighton

SASKATCHEWAN

Primrose L.
Cold L.
Doré L.
Smoothstone L.
Montreal L.
Cumberland L.
Moose L.

ALBERTA

Athabasca R.
Lesser Slave L.
Athabasca R.
Beaver R.
Meadow Lake
North Saskatchewan R.
Tobin L.
Lake Winnipegosis

Edmonton
Lloydminster
Shellbrook
Prince Albert
Nipawin
Saskatchewan R.
Carrot R.
Hudson Bay
Swan L.

Battle R.
North Battleford
Battleford
Melfort
Tisdale
Red Deer R.

Unity
Wilkie
Humboldt
Kelvington

Biggar
Saskatoon
Quill Lakes
Foam Lake
Kamsack

Kindersley
Rosetown
Watrous
Last Mountain L.
Yorkton

Calgary
Red Deer R.
Alsask
Outlook
Gardiner Dam
Melville
Esterhazy

Bow R.
Saskatchewan R.
Diefenbaker L.
Fort Qu'Appelle
Qu'Appelle R.
Assiniboine R.

South Saskatchewan R.
Herbert
Trans-Canada Hwy.
Regina
Grenfell
Trans-Canada Highway

Medicine Hat
Gull Lake
Swift Current
Moose Jaw
Old Wives L.
Weyburn
Carlyle

Maple Creek
Gravelbourg
Assiniboia
Souris R.

Val Marie
Estevan

Milk R.

UNITED STATES

B.C.

A 116° B 114° C 112° D 110° E 108° F 106° G 104° H 102° J 100° K
60° 1 58° 2 56° 3 54° 4 52° 5 50° 6
B 114° C 112° D 110° E 108° F 106° G 104° H 102° J

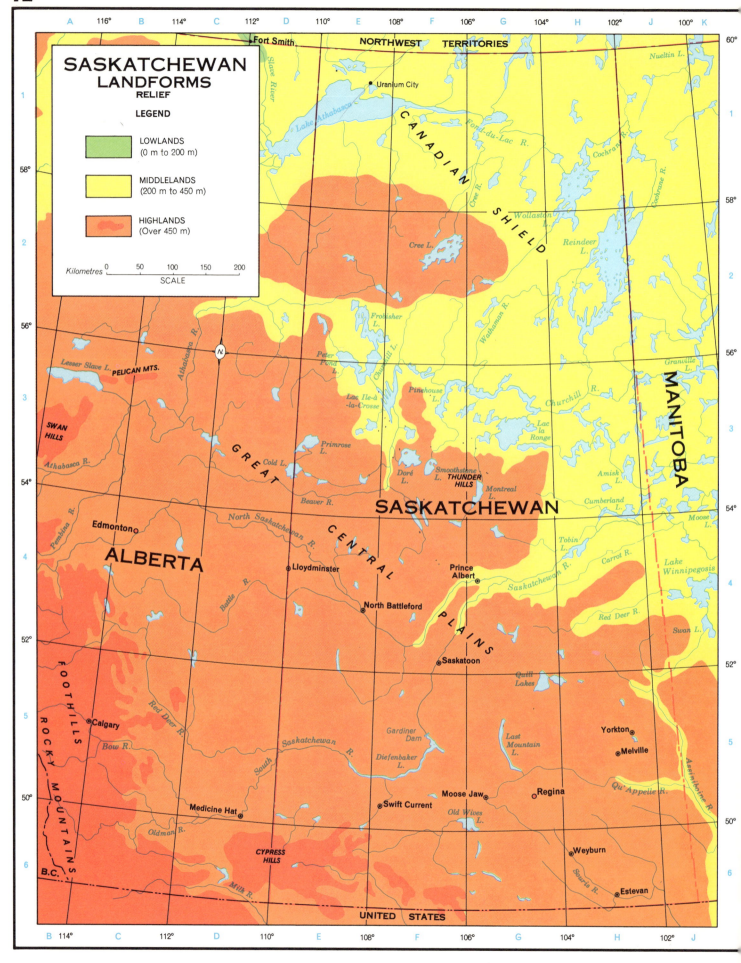

SASKATCHEWAN
LANDFORMS
RELIEF

LEGEND

LOWLANDS
(0 m to 200 m)

MIDDLELANDS
(200 m to 450 m)

HIGHLANDS
(Over 450 m)

Kilometres
0   50   100   150   200
SCALE

NORTHWEST   TERRITORIES

Fort Smith

Uranium City

Nueltin L.

Lake Athabasca

Fond-du-Lac R.

Cochrane R.

CANADIAN SHIELD

Wollaston L.

Cree R.

Cree L.

Reindeer L.

Slave River

Wathaman R.

Frobisher L.

Peter Pond L.

Churchill L.

Lac Ile-à-la-Crosse

Granville L.

PELICAN MTS.

Lesser Slave L.

Athabasca R.

Pinehouse L.

Churchill R.

MANITOBA

SWAN HILLS

Athabasca R.

N.

Primrose L.

Doré L.

Smoothstone L.

Lac la Ronge

Amisk L.

GREAT

Cold L.

THUNDER HILLS

Montreal L.

Cumberland L.

Moose L.

Beaver R.

SASKATCHEWAN

Penbina R.

North Saskatchewan R.

CENTRAL

Tobin L.

Edmonton

ALBERTA

Lloydminster

Prince Albert

Saskatchewan R.

Lake Winnipegosis

Battle R.

North Battleford

PLAINS

Carrot R.

Red Deer R.

Swan L.

Saskatoon

Quill Lakes

Calgary

Red Deer R.

Gardiner Dam

Last Mountain L.

Yorkton

Melville

FOOTHILLS

Bow R.

South Saskatchewan R.

Diefenbaker L.

Regina

Qu'Appelle R.

Assiniboine R.

ROCKY MOUNTAINS

Medicine Hat

Swift Current

Moose Jaw

Old Wives L.

Weyburn

CYPRESS HILLS

B.C.

Oldman R.

Milk R.

Souris R.

Estevan

UNITED   STATES

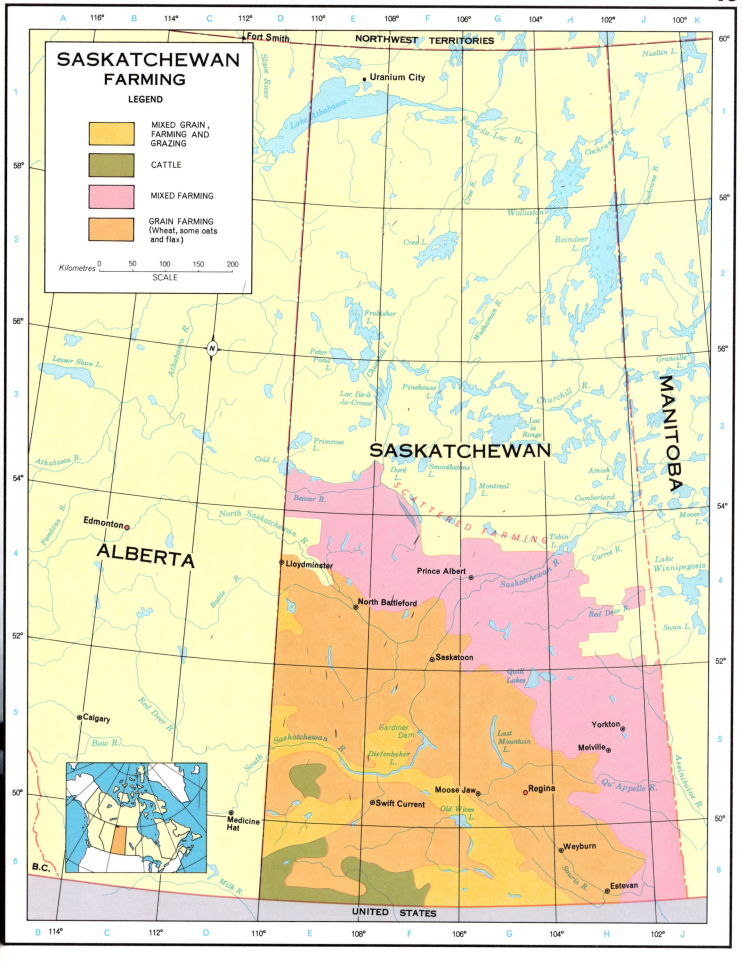

SASKATCHEWAN FARMING

LEGEND

- **MIXED GRAIN, FARMING AND GRAZING**
- **CATTLE**
- **MIXED FARMING**
- **GRAIN FARMING** (Wheat, some oats and flax)

Kilometres 0 50 100 150 200
SCALE

NORTHWEST TERRITORIES

Fort Smith

Uranium City

MANITOBA

SASKATCHEWAN

SCATTERED FARMING

ALBERTA

Edmonton

Lloydminster

Prince Albert

North Battleford

Saskatoon

Yorkton

Melville

Calgary

Gardiner Dam

Last Mountain L.

Diefenbaker L.

Moose Jaw

Regina

Swift Current

Old Wives L.

Weyburn

Medicine Hat

Estevan

B.C.

UNITED STATES

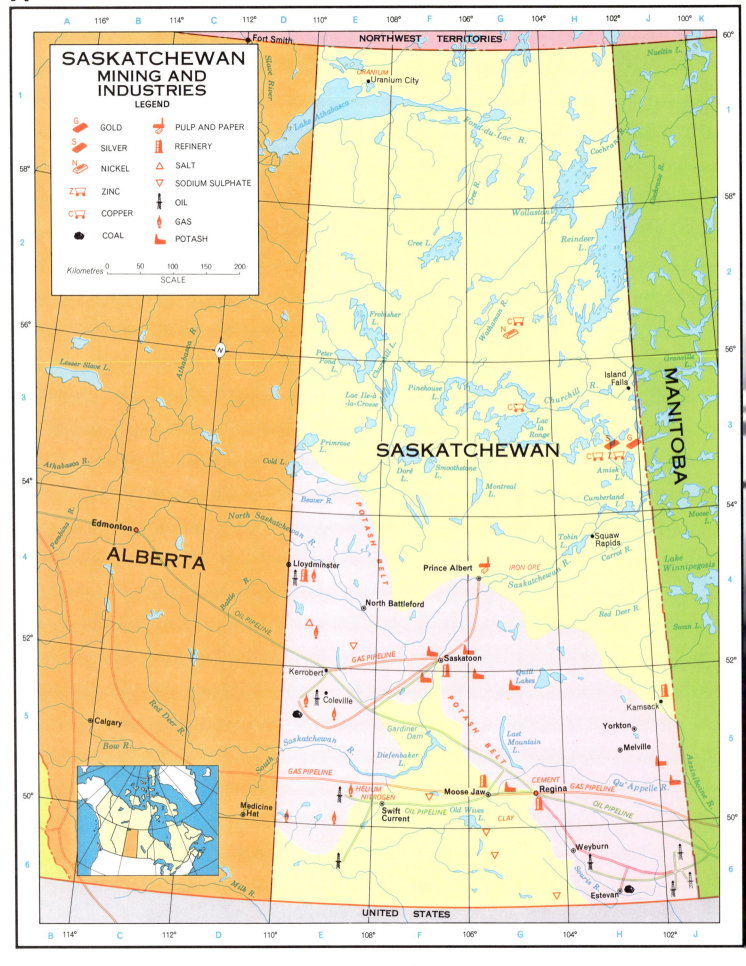

SASKATCHEWAN
MINING AND INDUSTRIES
LEGEND

G	GOLD		PULP AND PAPER
S	SILVER		REFINERY
N	NICKEL	△	SALT
Z	ZINC	▽	SODIUM SULPHATE
C	COPPER		OIL
●	COAL		GAS
			POTASH

Kilometres 0   50   100   150   200
SCALE

NORTHWEST TERRITORIES

Fort Smith

URANIUM

Uranium City

Slave River

Lake Athabasca

Fond-du-Lac R.

Nueltin L.

Cochrane R.

Granville L.

MANITOBA

Athabasca R.

Lesser Slave L.

Cree R.

Wollaston L.

Reindeer L.

Cree L.

Frobisher L.

Wathaman R.

N **C**

Peter Pond L.

Churchill L.

Pinehouse L.

Churchill R.

Island Falls

SASKATCHEWAN

C

Lac Ile-à-la-Crosse

Lac la Ronge

S **G**
C **Z**

Amisk L.

Primrose L.

Doré L.

Smoothstone L.

Montreal L.

Cumberland L.

Moose L.

Cold L.

Beaver R.

North Saskatchewan R.

Tobin L.

Squaw Rapids

Lake Winnipegosis

Athabasca R.

Pembina R.

Edmonton

ALBERTA

Battle R.

OIL PIPELINE

Lloydminster

North Battleford

△

Prince Albert

IRON ORE

Saskatchewan R.

Red Deer R.

Swan L.

▽

GAS PIPELINE

Kerrobert

Saskatoon

Quill Lakes

Kamsack

Red Deer R.

Coleville

●

Gardiner Dam

Last Mountain L.

Yorkton

Melville

Calgary

Red Deer R.

Bow R.

South Saskatchewan R.

Diefenbaker L.

POTASH BELT

Qu'Appelle R.

Assiniboine R.

GAS PIPELINE

HELIUM
NITROGEN

Moose Jaw

CEMENT

Regina

GAS PIPELINE

OIL PIPELINE

Medicine Hat

Swift Current

OIL PIPELINE

Old Wives L.

CLAY

▽

Weyburn

Milk R.

▽

Souris R.

UNITED STATES

Estevan

●

POTASH BELT

ALBERTA
TRANSPORTATION
LEGEND

- ⦿ PROVINCIAL CAPITALS
- ◉ MAJOR CITIES
- • OTHER CITIES AND TOWNS
- ⌇ POWER SITES
- ✈ MAJOR AIRPORTS
- ≈ MAJOR ROADS
- 〜 PRINCIPAL RAILWAYS
- —·—·— PROVINCIAL BOUNDARIES
- ——— INTERNATIONAL BOUNDARIES

Kilometres 0   50   100   150   200
SCALE

NORTHWEST TERRITORIES

BRITISH COLUMBIA

ALBERTA

SASKATCHEWAN

UNITED STATES

Fort Smith
Tazin L.
Lake Athabasca
Fort Chipewyan
Buffalo L.
Bistcho L.
Mackenzie Highway
Hay R.
Fort Vermilion
Peace R.
L. Claire
Cree L.
Wabasca R.
Athabasca R.
Fort McMurray
Frobisher L.
Fort St. John
Alaska Highway
Peace R.
Peace River
Utikuma L.
Lesser Slave L.
Peter Pond L.
Churchill L.
Lac Ile-à-la-Crosse
Dawson Creek
Smoky R.
Lac la Biche
Primrose L.
Grande Prairie
Athabasca R.
Athabasca
Cold L.
Doré L.
Prince George
Fraser R.
Pembina R.
North Saskatchewan R.
Beaver R.
Quesnel L.
Jasper
Drayton Valley
Edmonton
Vegreville
Lloydminster
Wetaskiwin
Camrose
Battle R.
Wainwright
North Battleford
Ponoka
Lacombe
Rocky Mountain House
Red Deer
Saskatchewan R.
Kicking Horse Pass
Drumheller
Red Deer R.
Trans-Canada Highway
Banff
Calgary
Bow R.
Turner Valley
High River
Trans-Canada Highway
Claresholm
Medicine Hat
Kimberley
Crowsnest Pass
Fort Macleod
Lethbridge
Kootenay L.
Kootenay R.
Oldman R.
Cranbrook
Pincher Creek
Milk R.

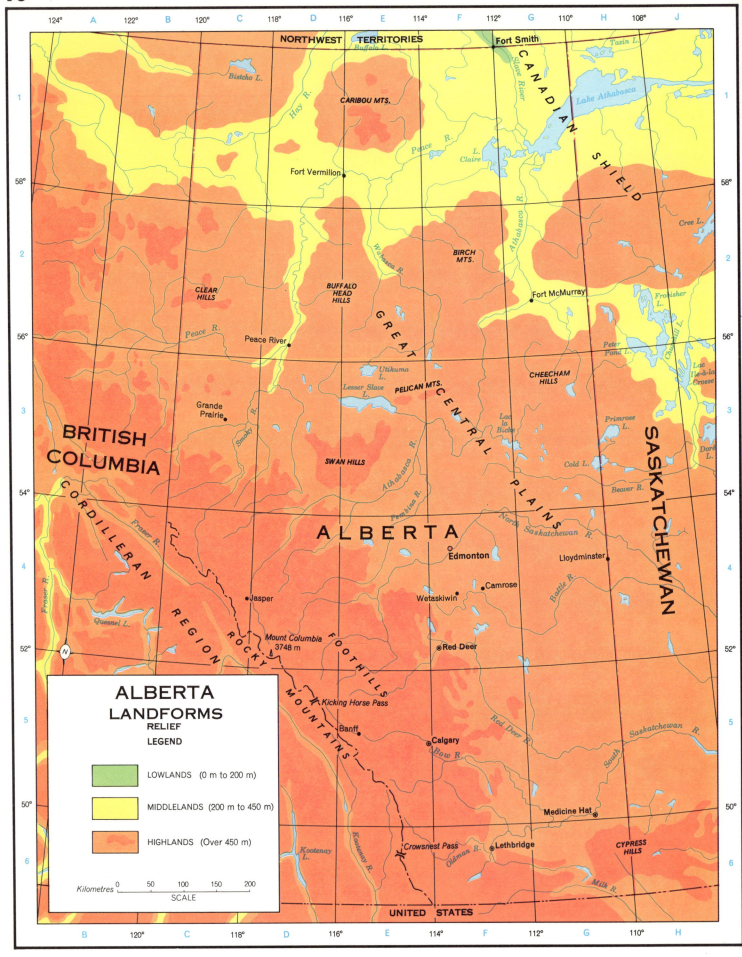

ALBERTA
LANDFORMS
RELIEF
LEGEND

LOWLANDS (0 m to 200 m)

MIDDLELANDS (200 m to 450 m)

HIGHLANDS (Over 450 m)

Kilometres 0   50   100   150   200
SCALE

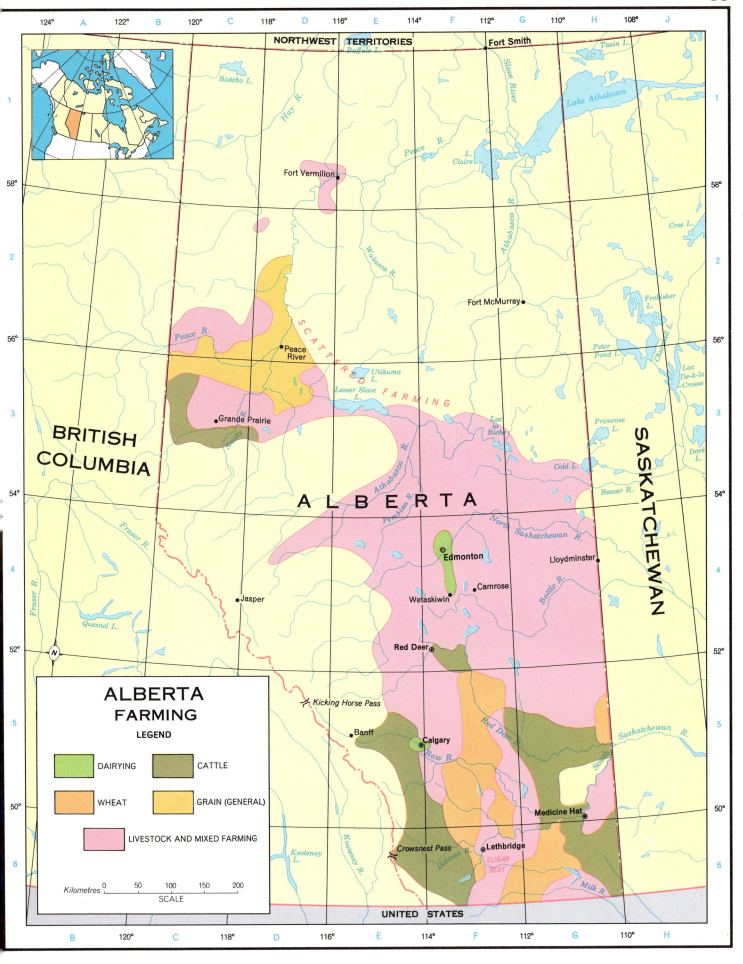

BRITISH
COLUMBIA

SASKATCHEWAN

A L B E R T A

SCATTERED FARMING

Fort Smith

Fort Vermilion

Fort McMurray

Peace
River

Grande Prairie

Edmonton

Lloydminster

Camrose

Wetaskiwin

Jasper

Red Deer

Kicking Horse Pass

Banff

Calgary

Medicine Hat

Crowsnest Pass

Lethbridge

SUGAR
BEET

UNITED STATES

ALBERTA
FARMING
LEGEND

- DAIRYING
- CATTLE
- WHEAT
- GRAIN (GENERAL)
- LIVESTOCK AND MIXED FARMING

Kilometres
0   50   100   150   200
SCALE

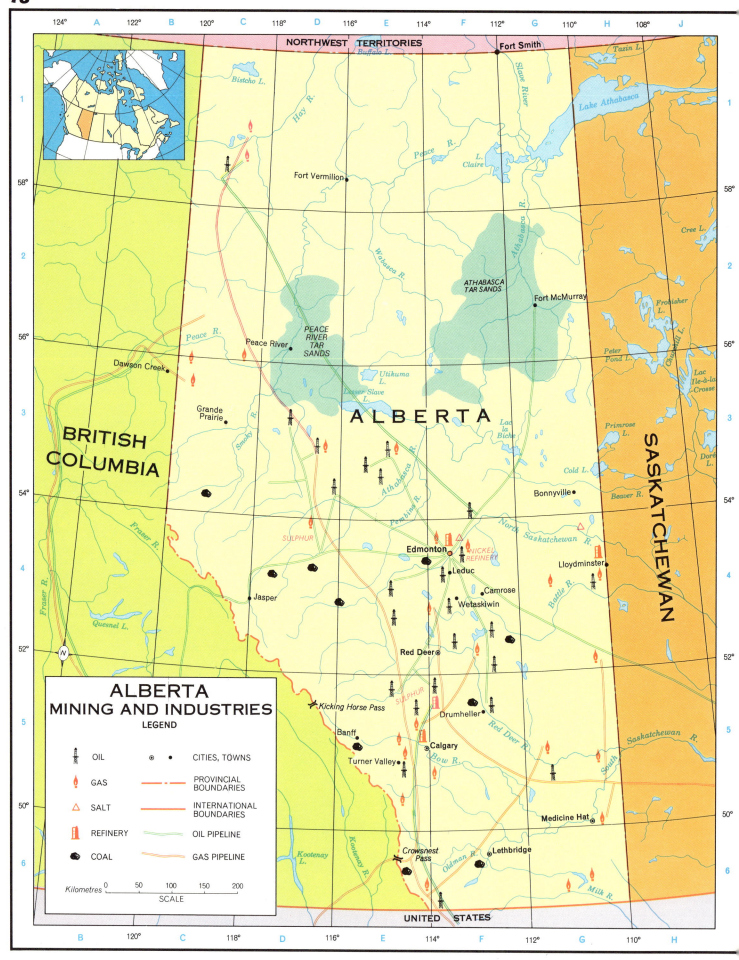

ALBERTA
MINING AND INDUSTRIES

LEGEND

OIL

GAS

SALT

REFINERY

COAL

⊙ • CITIES, TOWNS

PROVINCIAL BOUNDARIES

INTERNATIONAL BOUNDARIES

OIL PIPELINE

GAS PIPELINE

Kilometres 0 50 100 150 200
SCALE

BRITISH COLUMBIA

ALBERTA

SASKATCHEWAN

NORTHWEST TERRITORIES

UNITED STATES

Fort Smith
Buffalo L.
Slave River
Tazin L.
Lake Athabasca
Bistcho L.
Hay R.
Peace R.
L. Claire
Cree L.
Fort Vermilion
Wabasca R.
Athabasca R.
ATHABASCA TAR SANDS
Fort McMurray
Frobisher L.
Peace R.
Peace River
PEACE RIVER TAR SANDS
Peter Pond L.
Lac Ile-à-la-Crosse
Dawson Creek
Utikuma L.
Lesser Slave
Primrose L.
Doré L.
Grande Prairie
Smoky R.
Lac la Biche
Dore L.
Cold L.
Bonnyville
Beaver R.
SULPHUR
Athabasca R.
Pembina R.
North Saskatchewan R.
NICKEL REFINERY
Edmonton
Leduc
Lloydminster
Jasper
Camrose
Wetaskiwin
Battle R.
Red Deer
Fraser R.
Quesnel L.
Saskatchewan R.
SULPHUR
Kicking Horse Pass
Drumheller
Red Deer R.
Banff
Calgary
Turner Valley
Bow R.
South Saskatchewan R.
Medicine Hat
N
Kootenay L.
Kootenay R.
Crowsnest Pass
Oldman R.
Lethbridge
Milk R.
Fraser R.

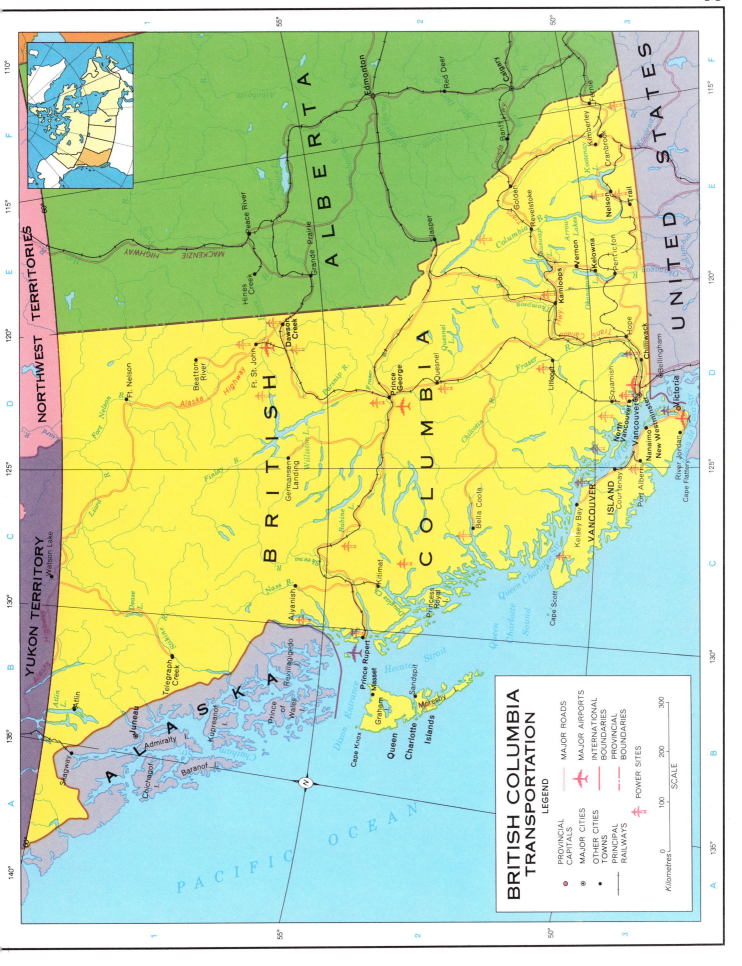

BRITISH COLUMBIA
TRANSPORTATION

LEGEND

● PROVINCIAL CAPITALS		—— MAJOR ROADS
⊙ MAJOR CITIES		✈ MAJOR AIRPORTS
• OTHER CITIES		—— INTERNATIONAL BOUNDARIES
• TOWNS		—— PROVINCIAL BOUNDARIES
—— PRINCIPAL RAILWAYS		✦ POWER SITES

SCALE

Kilometres 0   100   200   300

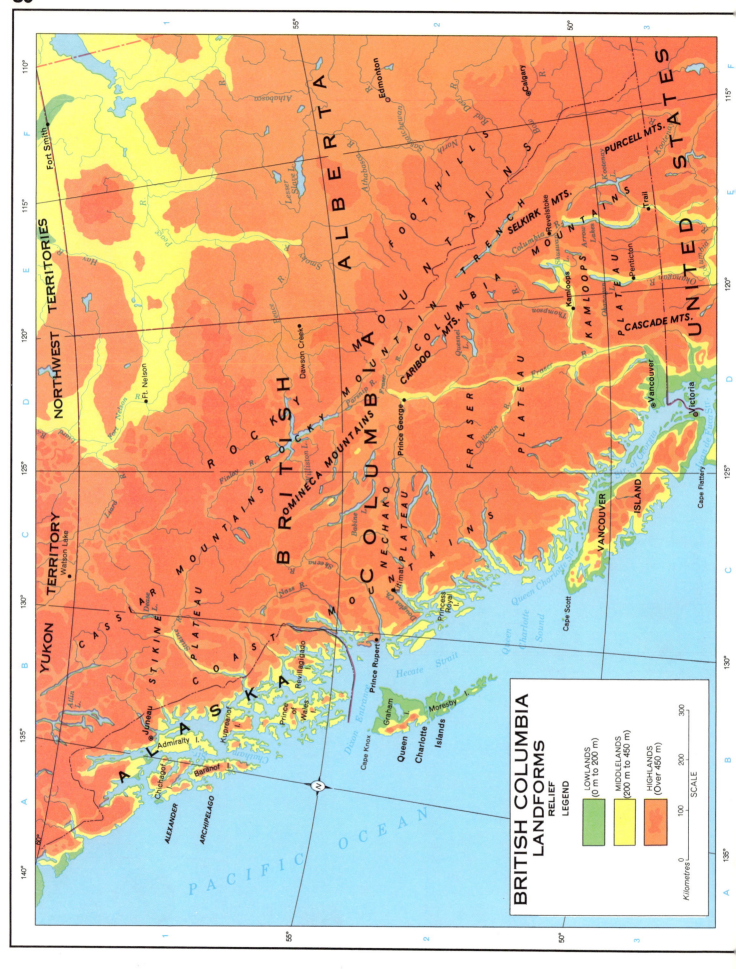

BRITISH COLUMBIA LANDFORMS

RELIEF LEGEND

LOWLANDS (0 m to 200 m)

MIDDLELANDS (200 m to 450 m)

HIGHLANDS (Over 450 m)

SCALE

Kilometres 0 100 200 300

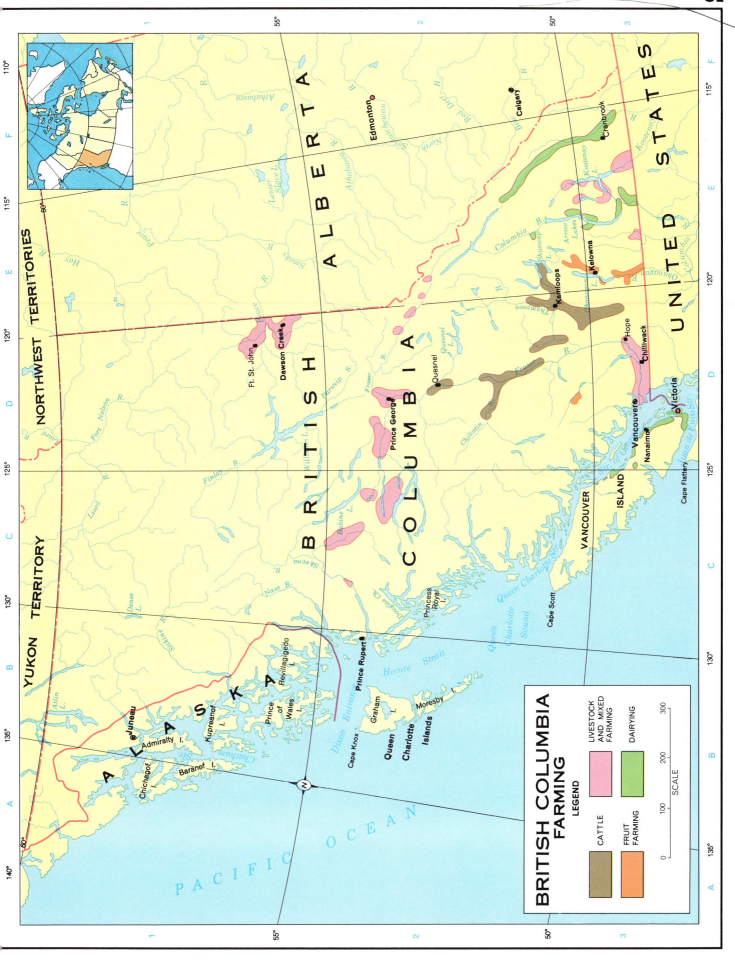

PACIFIC OCEAN

YUKON TERRITORY

NORTHWEST TERRITORIES

ALASKA

BRITISH COLUMBIA

ALBERTA

UNITED STATES

VANCOUVER ISLAND

Juneau
Admiralty I.
Chichagof I.
Baranof I.
Kupreanof I.
Prince of Wales I.
Revillagigedo I.
Prince Rupert
Graham I.
Moresby I.
Queen Charlotte Islands
Cape Knox
Princess Royal I.
Cape Scott
Cape Flattery
Victoria
Nanaimo
Vancouver
Chilliwack
Hope
Kamloops
Kelowna
Cranbrook
Calgary
Edmonton
Ft. St. John
Dawson Creek
Prince George
Quesnel

Atlin L.
Dease L.
Liard R.
Fort Nelson R.
Hay R.
Peace R.
Finlay R.
Parsnip R.
Williston L.
Nass R.
Skeena R.
Babine L.
Stikine R.
Chatham Str.
Dixon Entrance
Hecate Strait
Queen Charlotte Sound
Queen Charlotte Str.
Juan de Fuca Str.
Str. of Georgia
Douglas Ch.
Fraser R.
Chilcotin
Quesnel L.
Thompson R.
Shuswap L.
Arrow Lakes
Kootenay L.
Columbia R.
Okanagan R.
Athabasca R.
Lesser Slave L.
North Saskatchewan R.
Red Deer R.
Bow R.
Smoky R.

BRITISH COLUMBIA FARMING

LEGEND

- LIVESTOCK AND MIXED FARMING
- DAIRYING
- CATTLE
- FRUIT FARMING

SCALE
0 100 200 300

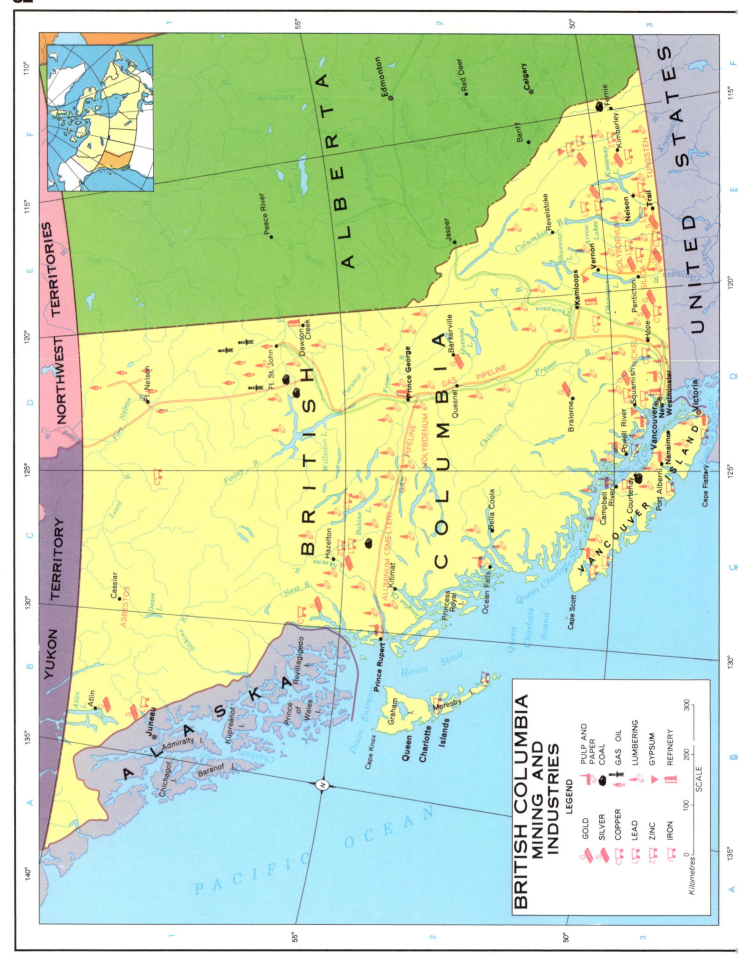

BRITISH COLUMBIA
MINING AND
INDUSTRIES

LEGEND

PULP AND PAPER
COAL
GAS OIL
LUMBERING
GYPSUM
REFINERY

G GOLD
S SILVER
COPPER
LEAD
Z ZINC
IRON

SCALE

Kilometres 0   100   200   300

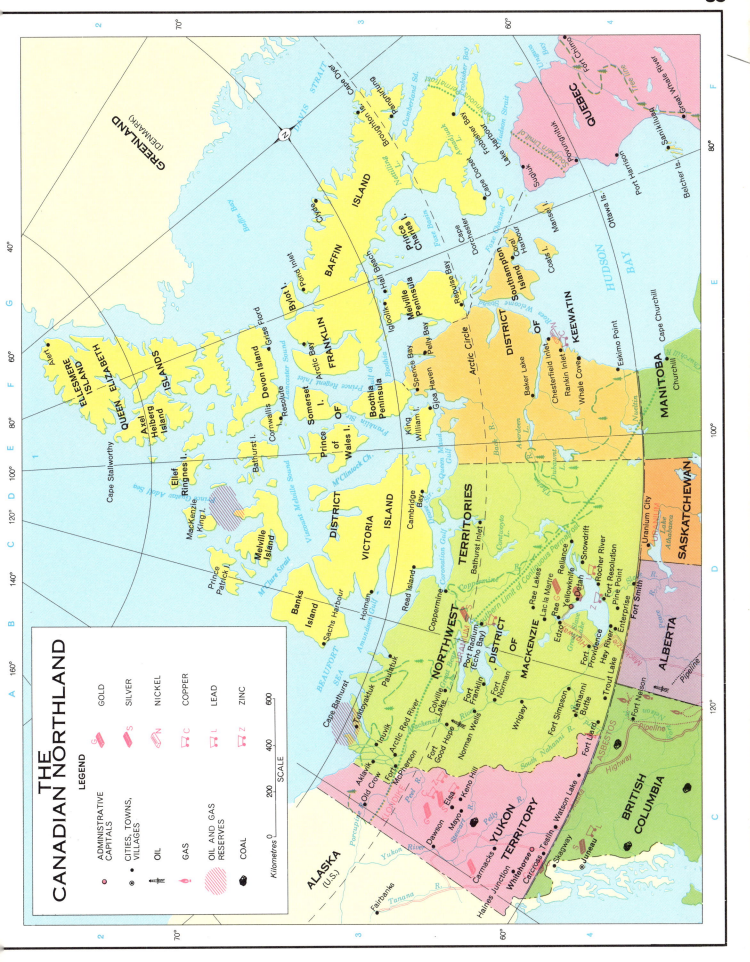

THE CANADIAN NORTHLAND

LEGEND

ADMINISTRATIVE CAPITALS

CITIES, TOWNS, VILLAGES

OIL

GAS

OIL AND GAS RESERVES

COAL

G GOLD	
S SILVER	
N NICKEL	
C COPPER	
L LEAD	
Z ZINC	

SCALE

Kilometres 0 200 400 600

GREENLAND (DENMARK)

QUEBEC

Fort Chimo
Leaf River
Great Whale River
Sanikiluaq
Povungnituk
Port Harrison
Belcher Is.
Ottawa Is.
Mansel I.
Coral Harbour
Coats I.
Southampton Island
Cape Dorchester
Lake Harbour
Frobisher Bay
Baffin Bay
Davis Strait
Cape Dyer
Pangnirtung
Cumberland Sd.
Broughton Is.

BAFFIN ISLAND

Clyde
Pond Inlet
Bylot I.
Arctic Bay
Hall Beach
Igloolik
Melville Peninsula
Repulse Bay
Spence Bay
Pelly Bay
Gjoa Haven

HUDSON BAY

Cape Churchill
Churchill
MANITOBA
Eskimo Point
Whale Cove
Rankin Inlet
Chesterfield Inlet
Baker Lake

DISTRICT OF KEEWATIN

Arctic Circle
Welcome Sound
Fox Channel
Foxe Basin

Prince Charles I.

DISTRICT OF FRANKLIN

Grise Fiord
Devon Island
Resolute
Cornwallis
Bathurst I.
Somerset I.
Prince of Wales I.
Boothia Peninsula
King William I.

Lancaster Sound
Prince Regent Inlet
Gulf of Boothia
Franklin Str.

ELLESMERE ISLAND
Alert
QUEEN ELIZABETH ISLANDS
Cape Stallworthy
Axel Heiberg Island
Ellef Ringnes I.
Amund Ringnes I.
MacKenzie King I.
Prince Gustaf Adolf Sea
Melville Island
Prince Patrick I.

VICTORIA ISLAND
Cambridge Bay
Read Island
Holman
Banks Island
Sachs Harbour

Viscount Melville Sound
M'Clintock Ch.
McClure Strait
Amundsen Gulf
Coronation Gulf
Dease Str.
Queen Maud Gulf
Back R.

BEAUFORT SEA
Cape Bathurst
Tuktoyaktuk
Paulatuk

DISTRICT OF MACKENZIE
NORTHWEST TERRITORIES
Bathurst Inlet
Contwoyto L.
Coppermine
Port Radium (Echo Bay)
Great Bear Lake
Rae Lakes
Snowdrift
Reliance
Rocher River
Yellowknife
Detah
Rae
Lac la Martre
Fort Resolution
Pine Point
Fort Smith
Enterprise
Hay River
Fort Providence
Edzo
Great Slave Lake

Inuvik
Aklavik
Fort McPherson
Arctic Red River
Colville Lake
Fort Good Hope
Norman Wells
Fort Norman
Fort Franklin
Wrigley
Nahanni Butte
Fort Simpson
Fort Liard
Trout Lake

Southern Limit of Continuous Permafrost
Mackenzie R.
South Nahanni R.
Liard R.

Aberdeen L.
Dubawnt L.
Nueltin L.
Thelon R.
Kasba L.

URANIUM CITY
Lake Athabasca
SASKATCHEWAN

ALBERTA
Fort Nelson
Peace R.
Pipeline
Slave R.

BRITISH COLUMBIA
ASBESTOS
Highway
Pipeline
Nelson R.

ALASKA (U.S.)
Fairbanks
Tanana R.
Old Crow
Porcupine R.
Yukon River

YUKON TERRITORY
Dawson
Mayo
Elsa
Keno Hill
Carmacks
Whitehorse
Haines Junction
Carcross
Teslin
Watson Lake
Skagway
Juneau
Pelly R.
Stewart R.
Peel R.
KLONDIKE

Baffin Bay

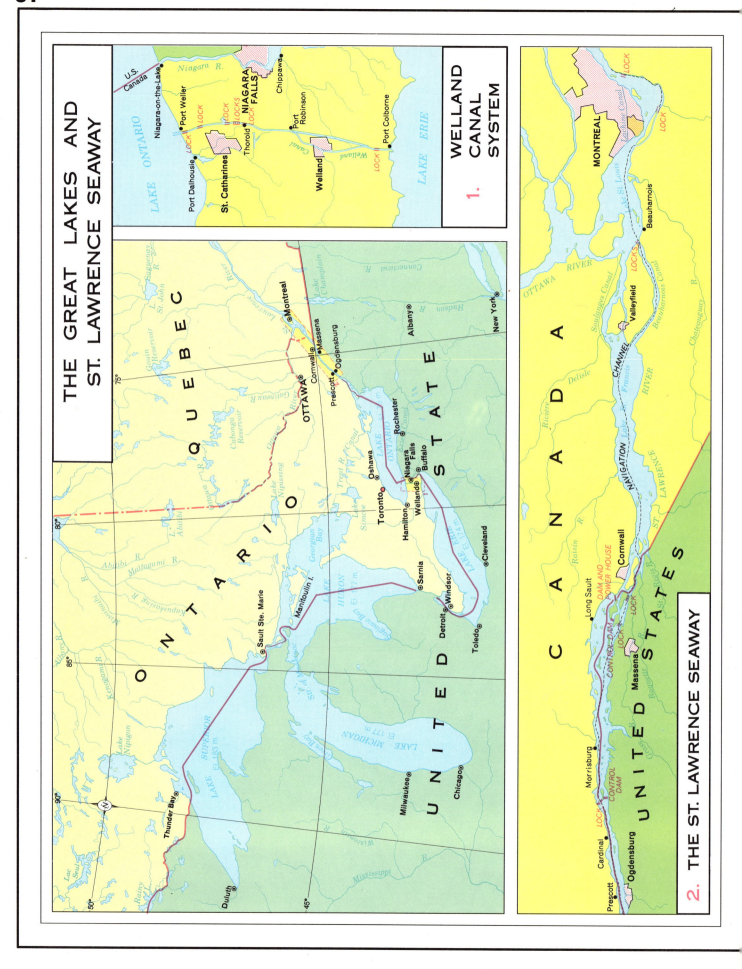

THE GREAT LAKES AND ST. LAWRENCE SEAWAY

1. WELLAND CANAL SYSTEM

2. THE ST. LAWRENCE SEAWAY

THE UNITED STATES
POLITICAL DIVISIONS
(EXCLUDING ALASKA AND HAWAII)

LEGEND

- ● CAPITAL CITIES
- ◉ STATE CAPITALS
- • OTHER CITIES, TOWNS
- ¦ STATE BOUNDARIES
- | INTERNATIONAL BOUNDARIES

SCALE

Kilometres 0   200   400   600

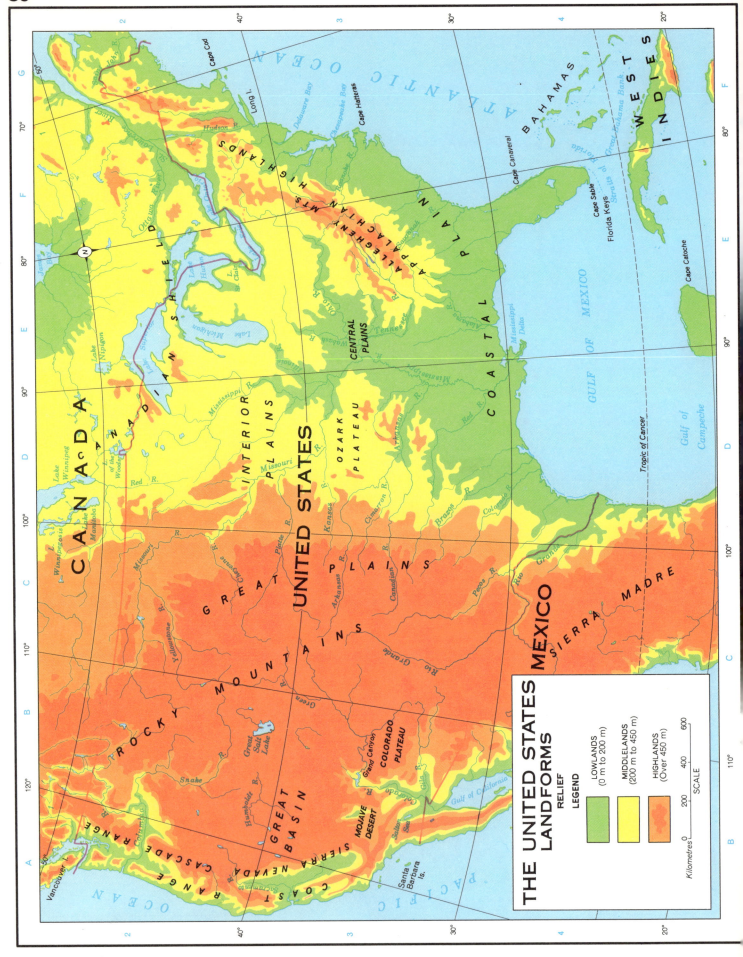

THE UNITED STATES
LANDFORMS

RELIEF
LEGEND

LOWLANDS (0 m to 200 m)	MIDDLELANDS (200 m to 450 m)	HIGHLANDS (Over 450 m)

SCALE

Kilometres 0   200   400   600

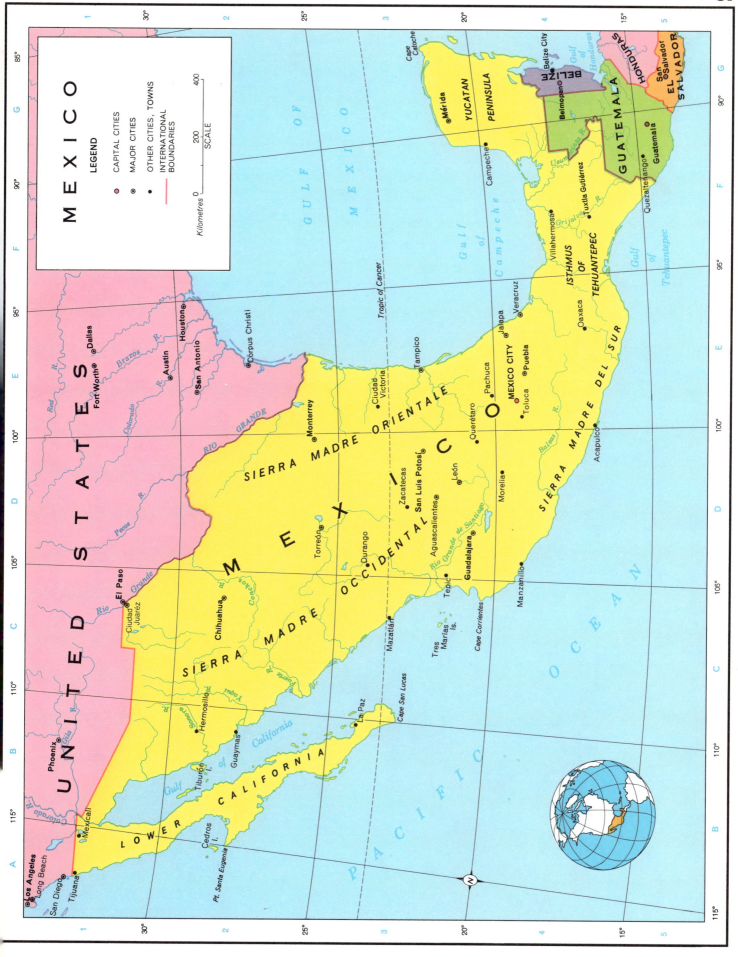

M E X I C O

LEGEND

- ● CAPITAL CITIES
- ◉ MAJOR CITIES
- ● OTHER CITIES, TOWNS
- ─── INTERNATIONAL BOUNDARIES

SCALE

Kilometres 0   200   400

U N I T E D   S T A T E S

Los Angeles
Long Beach
San Diego
Tijuana
Phoenix
Mexicali

Cedros I.
Pt. Santa Eugenia

LOWER CALIFORNIA

L O W E R   C A L I F O R N I A

Gulf of California

Tiburón I.
Guaymas
Hermosillo

La Paz
Cape San Lucas

Tres Marías Is.
Cape Corrientes

El Paso
Ciudad Juárez
Chihuahua

SIERRA MADRE OCCIDENTAL

SIERRA MADRE

Mazatlán
Tepic

Durango
Torreón

RIO GRANDE

Rio Grande

Red R.
Colorado R.
Pecos R.
Brazos R.

Fort Worth
Dallas
Austin
San Antonio
Houston
Corpus Christi

Monterrey

Ciudad Victoria

SIERRA MADRE ORIENTALE

Zacatecas
San Luis Potosí
Aguascalientes
León
Guadalajara
Manzanillo
Morelia

Tampico

Pachuca
Querétaro
MEXICO CITY
Toluca
Puebla

M E X I C O

Jalapa
Veracruz

Tropic of Cancer

GULF   OF   MEXICO

Gulf of Campeche

Cape Catoche

Mérida
YUCATAN PENINSULA

Campeche

Villahermosa

ISTHMUS OF TEHUANTEPEC

Oaxaca

SIERRA MADRE DEL SUR

Acapulco

Gulf of Tehuantepec

Tuxtla Gutiérrez

BELIZE
Belize City
Belmopan

Gulf of Honduras

HONDURAS

GUATEMALA
Guatemala
Quezaltenango

EL SALVADOR
San Salvador

P A C I F I C   O C E A N

N

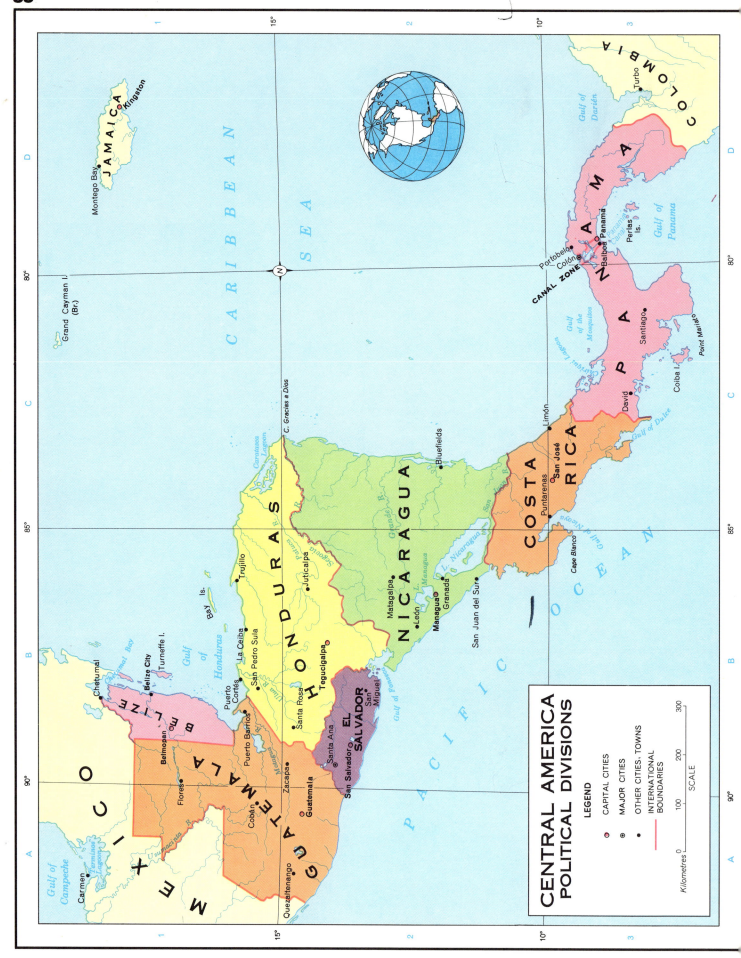

CENTRAL AMERICA
POLITICAL DIVISIONS

LEGEND

- CAPITAL CITIES
- MAJOR CITIES
- OTHER CITIES. TOWNS
- INTERNATIONAL BOUNDARIES

SCALE

Kilometres 0   100   200   300

JAMAICA
Kingston
Montego Bay

CARIBBEAN SEA

Grand Cayman I. (Br.)

COLOMBIA
Turbo
Gulf of Darién

PANAMA
Gulf of Panama
Perlas Is.
Panamá
Balboa
Portobelo
Colón
CANAL ZONE
Santiago
Coiba I.
Point Mariato
David
Gulf of the Mosquitos
Chiriquí Lagoon
Gulf of Dulce

COSTA RICA
Limón
San José
Puntarenas
Cape Blanco
Gulf of Nicoya

C. Gracias a Dios

Caratasca Lagoon

Bluefields

NICARAGUA
Grande R.
Segovia R.
Patuca R.
Matagalpa
León
Managua
Granada
L. Managua
L. Nicaragua
San Juan R.
San Juan del Sur

HONDURAS
Trujillo
Juticalpa
La Ceiba
San Pedro Sula
Puerto Cortés
Santa Rosa
Tegucigalpa
Bay Is.
Gulf of Honduras
Ulúa R.

EL SALVADOR
San Salvador
Santa Ana
San Miguel
Gulf of Fonseca

BELIZE
Belize City
Belmopan
Turneffe I.
Chetumal Bay

GUATEMALA
Flores
Cobán
Zacapa
Guatemala
Quezaltenango
Puerto Barrios
Usumacinta R.
Motagua R.
Chixoy R.

MEXICO
Carmen
Terminos Lagoon
Gulf of Campeche

PACIFIC OCEAN

N

80°
85°
90°
15°
10°

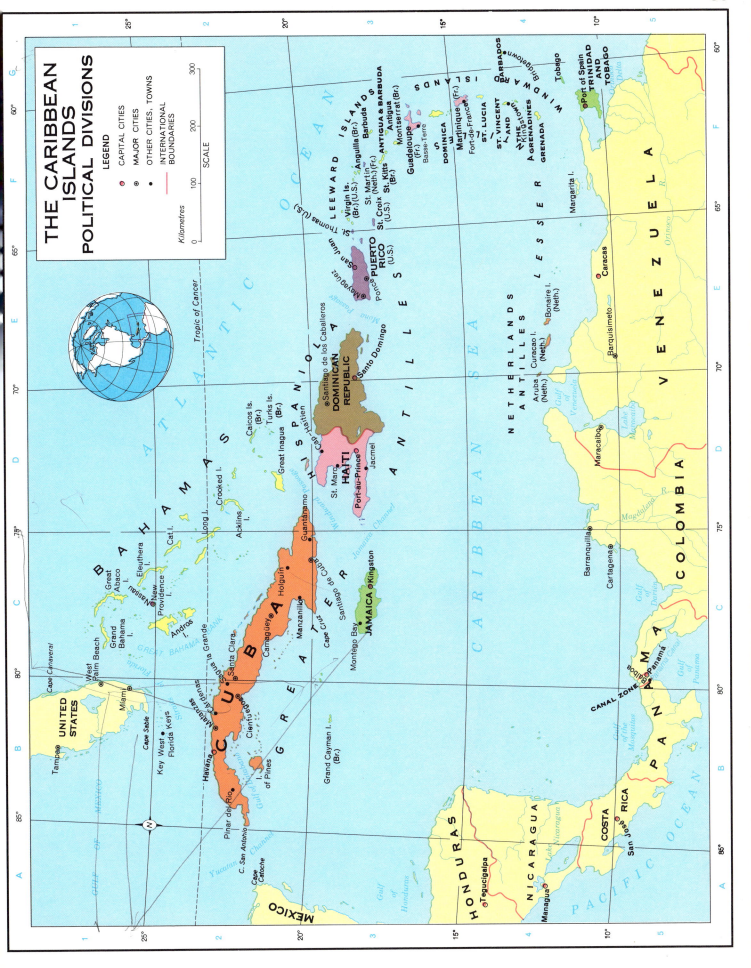

THE CARIBBEAN ISLANDS POLITICAL DIVISIONS

LEGEND

- ● CAPITAL CITIES
- ◉ MAJOR CITIES
- • OTHER CITIES, TOWNS
- — INTERNATIONAL BOUNDARIES

SCALE

Kilometres

0   100   200   300

SOUTH AMERICA
POLITICAL DIVISIONS

LEGEND

- ● CAPITAL CITIES
- ⊙ MAJOR CITIES
- • OTHER CITIES, TOWNS
- — INTERNATIONAL BOUNDARIES

Kilometres 0   400   800   1200
SCALE

SOUTH AMERICA
LANDFORMS
RELIEF

LEGEND

LOWLANDS
(0 m to 200 m)

MIDDLELANDS
(200 m to 450 m)

HIGHLANDS
(Over 450 m)

Kilometres 0   400   800   1200
SCALE

92

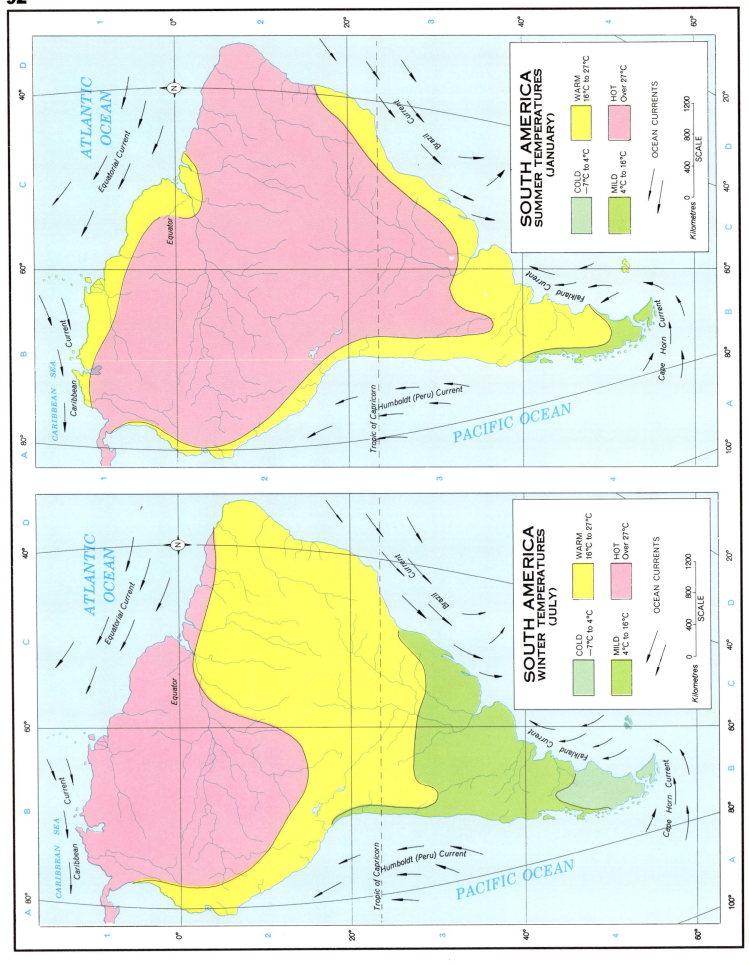

SOUTH AMERICA
SUMMER TEMPERATURES
(JANUARY)

COLD −7°C to 4°C
MILD 4°C to 16°C
WARM 16°C to 27°C
HOT Over 27°C
OCEAN CURRENTS

SCALE
Kilometres 0 400 800 1200

ATLANTIC OCEAN
Equatorial Current
Equator
CARIBBEAN SEA
Caribbean Current
Brazil Current
Falkland Current
Cape Horn Current
Tropic of Capricorn
Humboldt (Peru) Current
PACIFIC OCEAN

SOUTH AMERICA
WINTER TEMPERATURES
(JULY)

COLD −7°C to 4°C
MILD 4°C to 16°C
WARM 16°C to 27°C
HOT Over 27°C
OCEAN CURRENTS

SCALE
Kilometres 0 400 800 1200

ATLANTIC OCEAN
Equatorial Current
Equator
CARIBBEAN SEA
Caribbean Current
Brazil Current
Falkland Current
Cape Horn Current
Tropic of Capricorn
Humboldt (Peru) Current
PACIFIC OCEAN

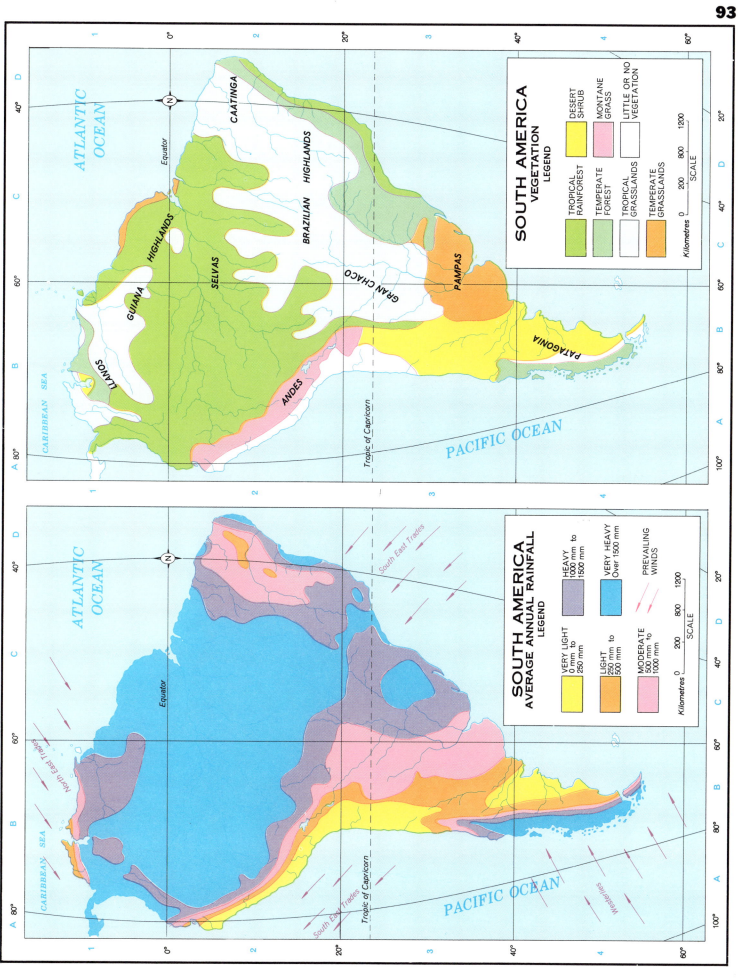

SOUTH AMERICA
VEGETATION
LEGEND

TROPICAL RAINFOREST
TEMPERATE FOREST
TROPICAL GRASSLANDS
TEMPERATE GRASSLANDS
DESERT SHRUB
MONTANE GRASS
LITTLE OR NO VEGETATION

Kilometres
0   200   400   800   1200
SCALE

ATLANTIC OCEAN
PACIFIC OCEAN
CARIBBEAN SEA
Equator
Tropic of Capricorn
CAATINGA
BRAZILIAN HIGHLANDS
GUIANA HIGHLANDS
SELVAS
LLANOS
ANDES
GRAN CHACO
PAMPAS
PATAGONIA

SOUTH AMERICA
AVERAGE ANNUAL RAINFALL
LEGEND

VERY LIGHT 0 mm to 250 mm
LIGHT 250 mm to 500 mm
MODERATE 500 mm to 1000 mm
HEAVY 1000 mm to 1500 mm
VERY HEAVY Over 1500 mm
PREVAILING WINDS

Kilometres
0   200   400   800   1200
SCALE

ATLANTIC OCEAN
PACIFIC OCEAN
CARIBBEAN SEA
Equator
Tropic of Capricorn
South East Trades
North East Trades
South East Trades
Westerlies

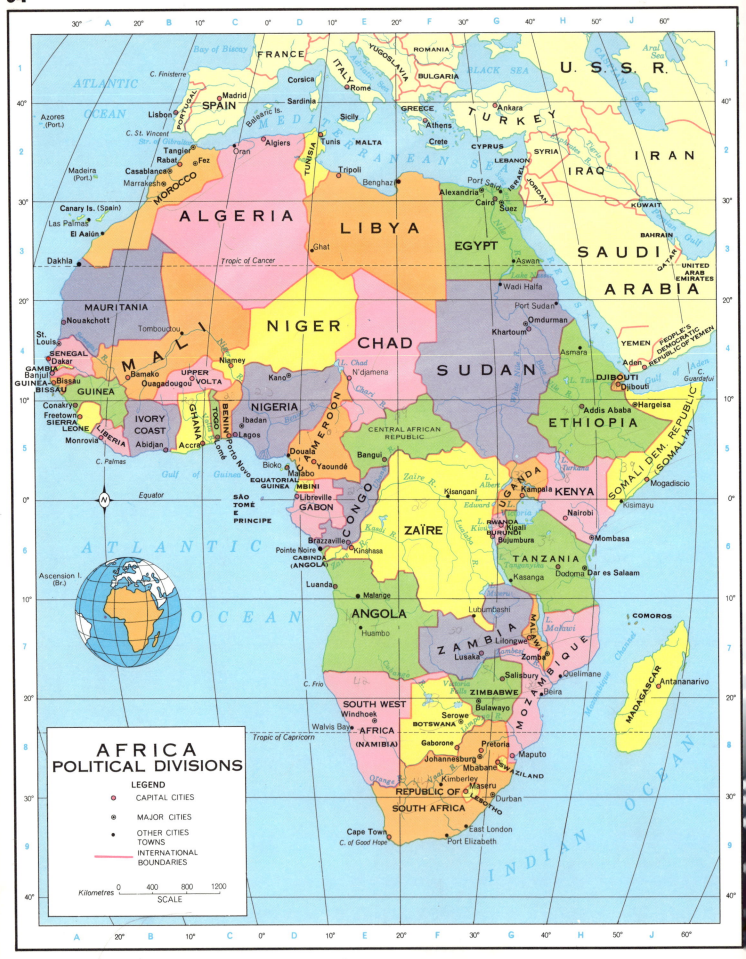

AFRICA
POLITICAL DIVISIONS

LEGEND

- ⬤ CAPITAL CITIES
- ⊙ MAJOR CITIES
- • OTHER CITIES TOWNS
- ▬ INTERNATIONAL BOUNDARIES

Kilometres 0   400   800   1200
SCALE

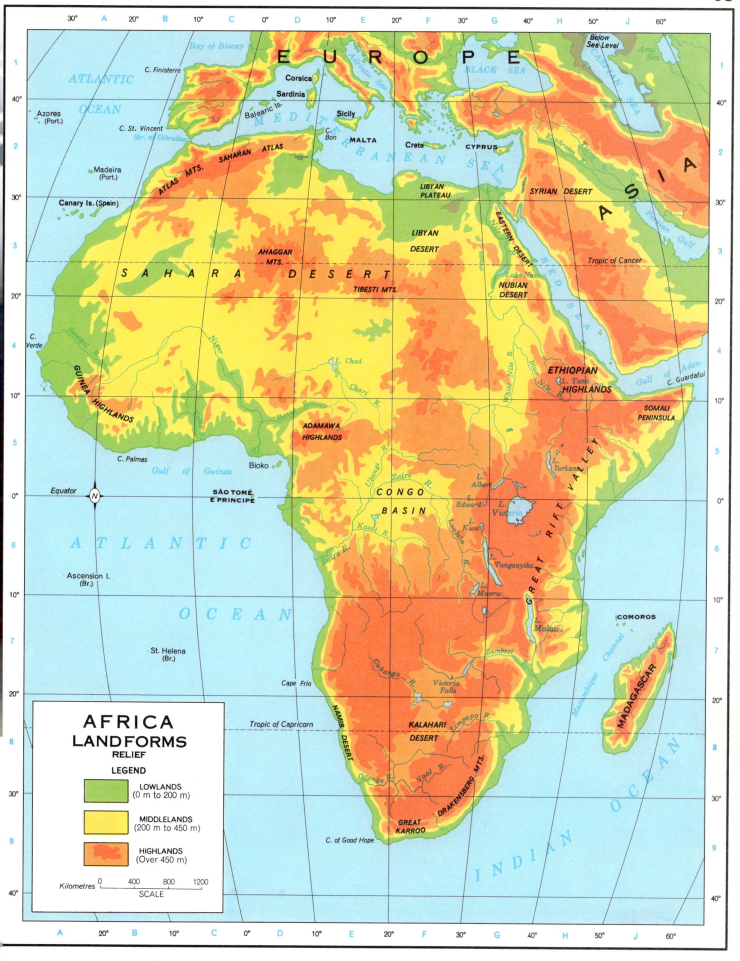

EUROPE

ASIA

ATLANTIC OCEAN

Bay of Biscay
C. Finisterre
Corsica
Sardinia
Balearic Is.
C. St. Vincent
Str. of Gibraltar
Sicily
MALTA
Crete
CYPRUS
Adriatic Sea
BLACK SEA
Below Sea Level
Aral Sea
CASPIAN SEA
Azores (Port.)
Madeira (Port.)
Canary Is. (Spain)
ATLAS MTS.
SAHARAN ATLAS
MEDITERRANEAN SEA
C. Bon
LIBYAN PLATEAU
SYRIAN DESERT
Euphrates R.
Tigris R.
Persian Gulf
AHAGGAR MTS.
SAHARA DESERT
LIBYAN DESERT
TIBESTI MTS.
NUBIAN DESERT
Suez Canal
EASTERN DESERT
RED SEA
Tropic of Cancer
Lake Nasser
C. Verde
Senegal R.
Niger R.
L. Chad
Chari R.
GUINEA HIGHLANDS
C. Palmas
Bioko
SÃO TOMÉ E PRINCIPE
ADAMAWA HIGHLANDS
Benue R.
Volta R.
ETHIOPIAN HIGHLANDS
L. Tana
White Nile R.
Blue Nile R.
Nile R.
Gulf of Aden
C. Guardafui
SOMALI PENINSULA
Equator
ATLANTIC OCEAN
Zaire R.
Ubangi R.
CONGO BASIN
Kasai R.
Lualaba R.
L. Albert
L. Edward
L. Kivu
L. Victoria
L. Turkana
GREAT RIFT VALLEY
Ascension I. (Br.)
St. Helena (Br.)
L. Tanganyika
L. Mweru
L. Malawi
COMOROS
Cape Frio
Cubango R.
Zambezi R.
Victoria Falls
Mozambique Channel
MADAGASCAR
Tropic of Capricorn
NAMIB DESERT
KALAHARI DESERT
Limpopo R.
Vaal R.
Orange R.
DRAKENSBERG MTS.
GREAT KARROO
C. of Good Hope
INDIAN OCEAN

AFRICA
LANDFORMS
RELIEF
LEGEND

LOWLANDS	(0 m to 200 m)
MIDDLELANDS	(200 m to 450 m)
HIGHLANDS	(Over 450 m)

Kilometres 200 400 800 1200
SCALE

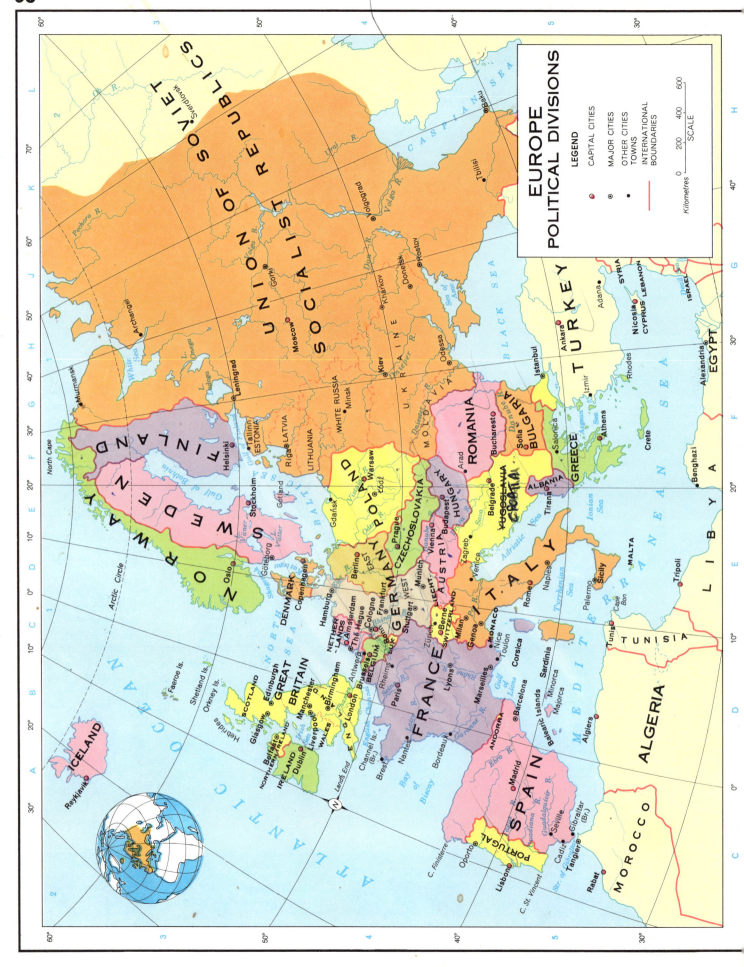

96

EUROPE POLITICAL DIVISIONS

LEGEND

- ⊙ CAPITAL CITIES
- ◉ MAJOR CITIES
- • OTHER CITIES TOWNS
- | INTERNATIONAL BOUNDARIES

Kilometres
0   200   400   600
SCALE

UNION OF SOVIET SOCIALIST REPUBLICS

Sverdlovsk

Ob R.
Irtysh R.
Ural R.

Pechora R.

Archangel

Murmansk

White Sea

L. Onega
L. Ladoga

Leningrad

Moscow

Gorki

Volga R.
Don R.

Volgograd

Rostov

Donetsk

Kharkov

Kiev

Dnieper R.

Odessa

CASPIAN SEA

Baku

Tbilisi

BLACK SEA

Istanbul

Ankara

TURKEY

Izmir

Adana

SYRIA

Nicosia **CYPRUS** **LEBANON**

ISRAEL

Rhodes

Athens

Aegean Sea

Salonica

Crete

GREECE

Benghazi

Alexandria

EGYPT

Tripoli

LIBYA

FINLAND

Helsinki

North Cape

Gulf of Bothnia

NORWAY

SWEDEN

Oslo

Stockholm

Göteborg

Vänern
Vättern

Gotland

North Cape

Arctic Circle

ICELAND

Reykjavik

ATLANTIC OCEAN

Faeroe Is.

Shetland Is.

Orkney Is.

Hebrides

SCOTLAND

Glasgow   Edinburgh

GREAT BRITAIN

Belfast

NORTHERN IRELAND

IRELAND

Dublin

Manchester

Liverpool

WALES

Birmingham

ENGLAND

London

Land's End

Channel Is. (Br.)

English Channel

Brest

Nantes

Bay of Biscay

Bordeaux

C. Finisterre

Oporto

PORTUGAL

Lisbon

C. St. Vincent

Cadiz

Seville

SPAIN

Madrid

Barcelona

ANDORRA

Ebro R.

Guadalquivir R.

Guadiana R.

Gibraltar (Br.)

Tangier

Rabat

MOROCCO

Str. of Gibraltar

Algiers

ALGERIA

Tunis

TUNISIA

Balearic Islands

Minorca

Majorca

MEDITERRANEAN SEA

Sardinia

Corsica

C. Bon

MALTA

Sicily

Palermo

Naples

Tyrrhenian Sea

Rome

ITALY

Genoa

Milan

Venice

Adriatic Sea

Ionian Sea

Tirana

ALBANIA

YUGOSLAVIA CROATIA

Zagreb

Sava R.

Belgrade

HUNGARY

Budapest

Vienna

AUSTRIA

Munich

LIECHT.

Berne

SWITZERLAND

Zürich

MONACO

Nice

Toulon

Marseilles

Gulf of Lions

Lyons

Rhône R.

FRANCE

Paris

Rheims

Seine R.
Loire R.
Garonne R.

DENMARK

Copenhagen

Skagerrak

NORTH SEA

Hamburg

NETHER-LANDS

Amsterdam

The Hague

BELGIUM

Brussels

Antwerp

Cologne

Frankfurt

WEST GERMANY

EAST GERMANY

Berlin

Elbe R.
Rhine R.

Stuttgart

CZECHOSLOVAKIA

Prague

POLAND

Warsaw

Łódź

Gdańsk

Vistula R.
Oder R.

ESTONIA

Tallinn

LATVIA

Riga

LITHUANIA

WHITE RUSSIA

Minsk

U K R A I N E

Dniester R.
Danube R.

MOLDAVIA

ROMANIA

Bucharest

Arad

BULGARIA

Sofia

Balearic

Genua

Baltic Sea

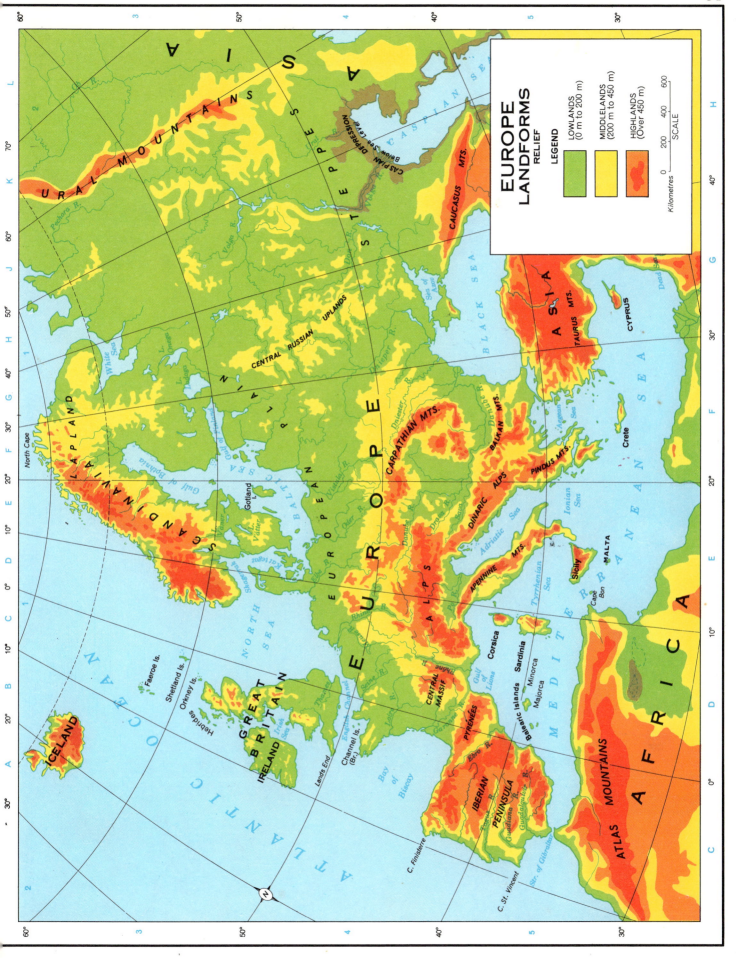

EUROPE LANDFORMS

RELIEF

LEGEND

LOWLANDS (0 m to 200 m)

MIDDLELANDS (200 m to 450 m)

HIGHLANDS (Over 450 m)

SCALE

Kilometres 0 200 400 600

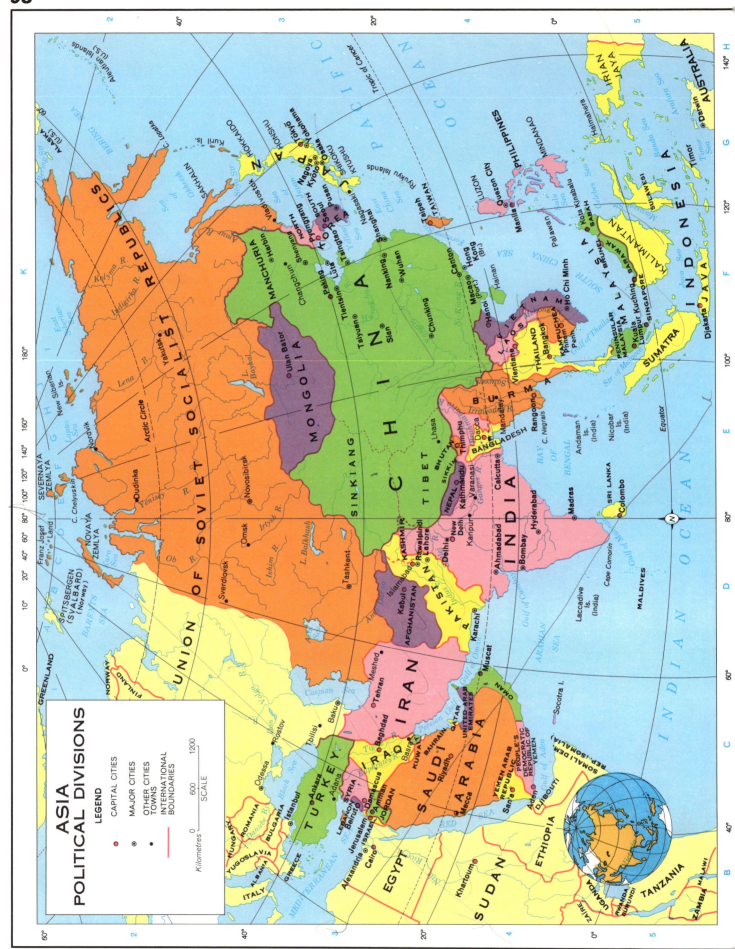

ASIA
POLITICAL DIVISIONS

LEGEND

⊙ CAPITAL CITIES
◉ MAJOR CITIES
• OTHER CITIES
  TOWNS
— INTERNATIONAL
  BOUNDARIES

SCALE
0   600   1200
Kilometres

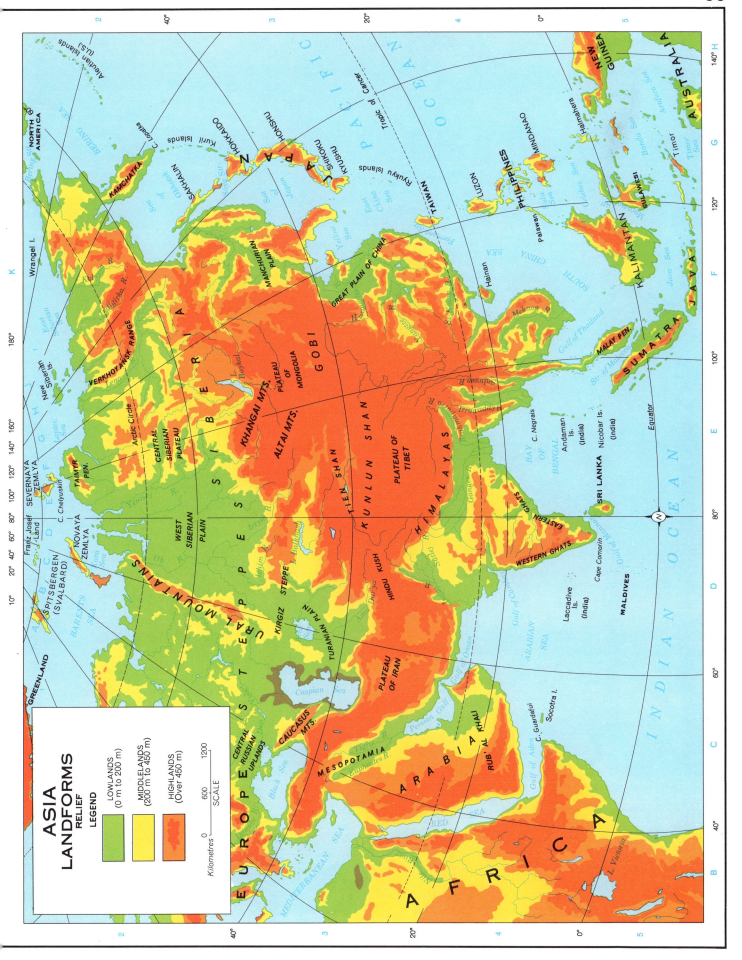

ASIA
LANDFORMS
RELIEF
LEGEND

LOWLANDS
(0 m to 200 m)

MIDDLELANDS
(200 m to 450 m)

HIGHLANDS
(Over 450 m)

SCALE

1200

600

0

Kilometres

NORTH
AMERICA

Aleutian Islands
(U.S.)

Wrangel I.

KAMCHATKA
C. Lopatka
Kuril Islands
SAKHALIN
HOKKAIDO
HONSHU
J A P A N
SHIKOKU
KYUSHU
Ryukyu Islands

BERING SEA

Sea of Okhotsk

Sea of Japan

East China Sea

Tropic of Cancer

TAIWAN
Formosa Str.

PACIFIC

OCEAN

NEW GUINEA
AUSTRALIA

PHILIPPINES
MINDANAO
LUZON
Halmahera
Banda Sea
Timor
Arafura Sea
Timor Sea

Celebes Sea
SULAWESI
KALIMANTAN
JAVA
Java Sea
SUMATRA
MALAY PEN.

SOUTH CHINA SEA
Hainan
Gulf of Thailand
Palawan
Sulu Sea

Mekong R.
Str. of Malacca
Andaman Is. (India)
Nicobar Is. (India)
C. Negrais

BAY OF BENGAL

SRI LANKA
Cape Comorin
Laccadive Is. (India)
MALDIVES

VERKHOYANSK RANGE
CENTRAL SIBERIAN PLATEAU
S I B E R I A
Arctic Circle
Lena
L. Baykal
MANCHURIAN PLAIN
GREAT PLAIN OF CHINA
Yellow Sea
Yellow R.
GOBI
PLATEAU OF MONGOLIA
KHANGAI MTS.
ALTAI MTS.
TIEN SHAN
KUNLUN SHAN
PLATEAU OF TIBET
HIMALAYAS
Yangtze R.
Salween R.
Brahmaputra R.
Irrawaddy R.
Ganges R.
EASTERN GHATS
WESTERN GHATS

TAIMYR PEN.
SEVERNAYA ZEMLYA
C. Chelyuskin
NOVAYA ZEMLYA
Kara Sea
Yenisey R.
Ob R.
WEST SIBERIAN PLAIN
Irtysh R.
L. Balkash
STEPPES
KIRGIZ STEPPE
Amu Dar'ya
Syr Dar'ya
Chu R.
Tarim R.
TURANIAN PLAIN
HINDU KUSH

GREENLAND
Franz Josef Land
SPITSBERGEN (SVALBARD)
BARENTS SEA
E U R O P E
URAL MOUNTAINS
Volga R.
Ural R.
Caspian Sea
CENTRAL RUSSIAN UPLANDS
CAUCASUS MTS.
Black Sea
MEDITERRANEAN SEA
MESOPOTAMIA
Tigris R.
Euphrates R.
Persian Gulf
PLATEAU OF IRAN
Gulf of Oman
ARABIAN SEA
Gulf of Aden
Socotra I.
C. Guardafui
A R A B I A
RUB' AL KHALI
RED SEA
AFRICA
L. Victoria

INDIAN

OCEAN

Equator

N

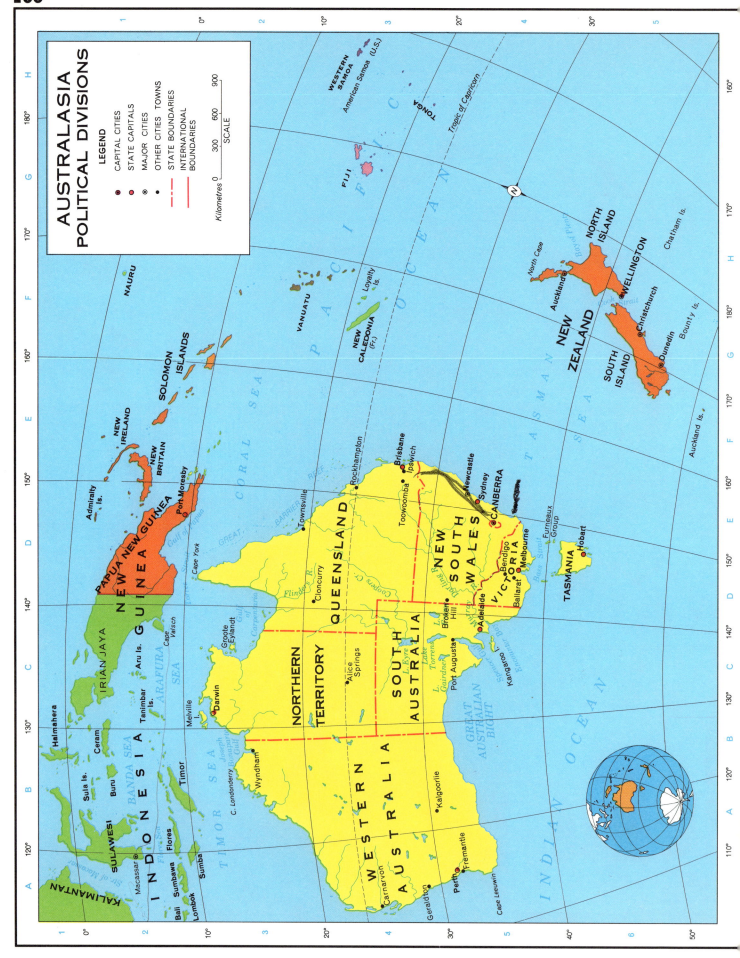

AUSTRALASIA POLITICAL DIVISIONS

LEGEND

- CAPITAL CITIES
- STATE CAPITALS
- MAJOR CITIES
- OTHER CITIES TOWNS
- STATE BOUNDARIES
- INTERNATIONAL BOUNDARIES

SCALE

Kilometres 0 300 600 900

PACIFIC OCEAN

WESTERN SAMOA
American Samoa (U.S.)

TONGA

Tropic of Capricorn

FIJI

NAURU

VANUATU

Loyalty Is.
NEW CALEDONIA (Fr.)

SOLOMON ISLANDS

NEW IRELAND
NEW BRITAIN

Admiralty Is.
PAPUA NEW GUINEA
Port Moresby

Gulf of Papua

Cape Valsch

IRIAN JAYA

Halmahera

Ceram
Sula Is.
Buru

BANDA SEA

Tanimbar
Aru Is.

ARAFURA SEA

Macassar
SULAWESI
INDONESIA

Bali Sumbawa Flores
Lombok Sumba

Str. of Macassar

KALIMANTAN

TIMOR SEA
Timor

Melville I.

C. Londonderry
Wyndham
Joseph Bonaparte Gulf

Darwin

Groote Eylandt
Gulf of Carpentaria

NORTHERN TERRITORY

Alice Springs

WESTERN AUSTRALIA

Carnarvon
Geraldton
Perth
Fremantle
Cape Leeuwin

Kalgoorlie

GREAT AUSTRALIAN BIGHT

INDIAN OCEAN

SOUTH AUSTRALIA

L. Eyre
L. Torrens
L. Gairdner
Port Augusta
Lake
Kangaroo I.
Encounter B.

Spencer G.

QUEENSLAND

Cape York
Cook

GREAT BARRIER REEF

Townsville

Flinders R.
Cloncurry

Coopers Cr.

Rockhampton

Brisbane
Ipswich
Toowoomba

CORAL SEA

NEW SOUTH WALES

Darling R.

Broken Hill
Adelaide

VICTORIA
Bendigo
Ballarat
Melbourne

Newcastle
Sydney
CANBERRA

Furneaux Group

Bass Strait
TASMANIA
Hobart

TASMAN SEA

NEW ZEALAND

North Cape
Bay of Plenty
NORTH ISLAND
Auckland
Cook Strait
WELLINGTON
Christchurch
SOUTH ISLAND
Dunedin
Bounty Is.

Chatham Is.

Auckland Is.

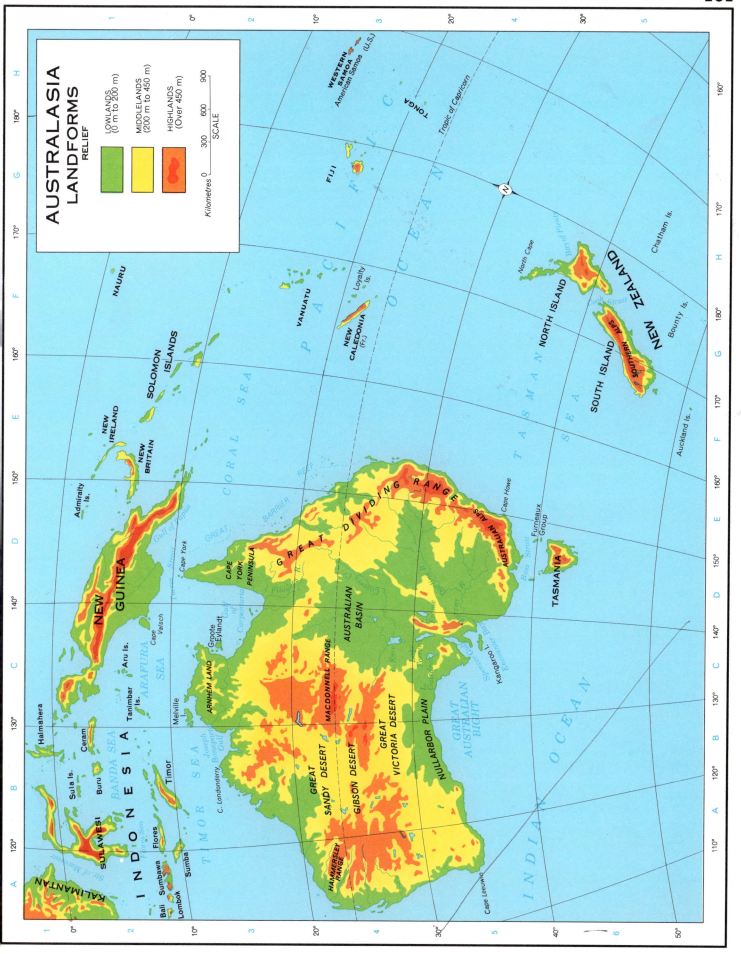

AUSTRALASIA
LANDFORMS
RELIEF

LOWLANDS
(0 m to 200 m)

MIDDLELANDS
(200 m to 450 m)

HIGHLANDS
(Over 450 m)

SCALE

Kilometres
0   300   600   900

P A C I F I C   O C E A N

WESTERN SAMOA (U.S.)
American Samoa

TONGA

Tropic of Capricorn

FIJI

VANUATU
NEW CALEDONIA (Fr.)
Loyalty Is.

North Cape
Bay of Plenty
Chatham Is.
Cook Strait
NORTH ISLAND
SOUTH ISLAND
SOUTHERN ALPS
NEW ZEALAND
Bounty Is.
Auckland Is.

NAURU

NEW IRELAND
NEW BRITAIN
Admiralty Is.
SOLOMON ISLANDS

NEW GUINEA

CORAL SEA
GREAT BARRIER REEF
Gulf of Papua
Torres Strait
Cape York

TASMAN SEA

Cape Howe
AUSTRALIAN ALPS
Furneaux Group
Bass Strait
TASMANIA

INDONESIA
Halmahera
Sula Is.
Ceram
Buru
SULAWESI
KALIMANTAN
Flores
Bali
Lombok
Sumbawa
Sumba
Timor
Tanimbar Is.
Aru Is.
Cape Valsch

BANDA SEA
Flores Sea
Str. of Makassar

ARAFURA SEA

TIMOR SEA
C. Londonderry
Joseph Bonaparte Gulf
Melville I.
Groote Eylandt
Gulf of Carpentaria

ARNHEM LAND

CAPE YORK PENINSULA

GREAT DIVIDING RANGE

AUSTRALIAN BASIN

MACDONNELL RANGE

GREAT SANDY DESERT

GIBSON DESERT

GREAT VICTORIA DESERT

NULLARBOR PLAIN

GREAT AUSTRALIAN BIGHT

Spencer Gulf
Kangaroo I.

HAMMERSLEY RANGE

Cape Leeuwin

I N D I A N   O C E A N

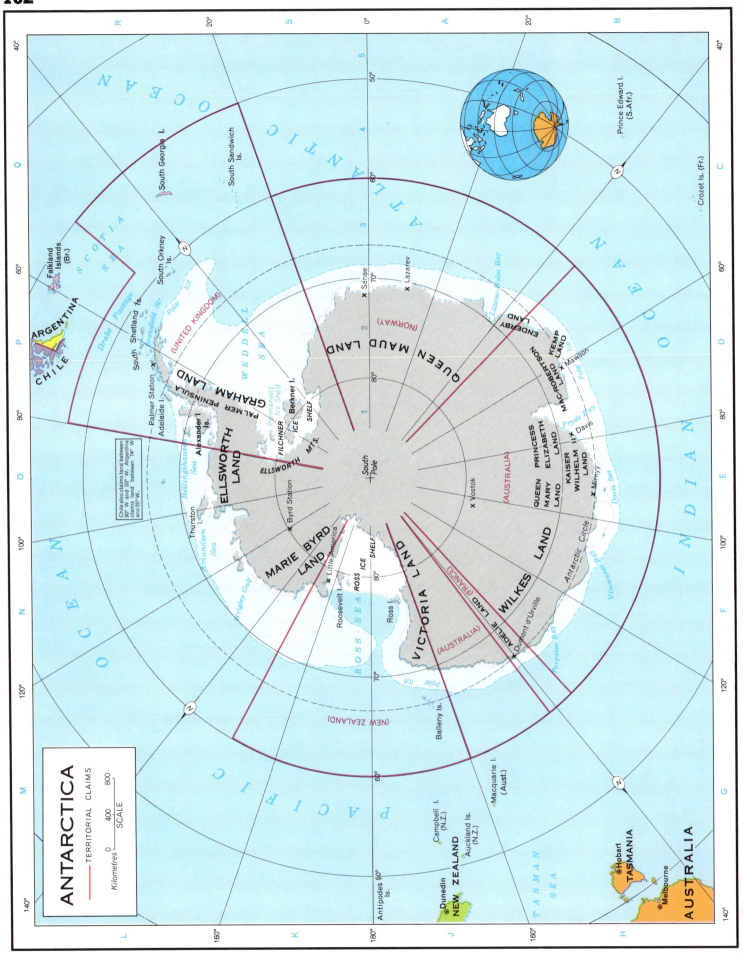

ANTARCTICA

TERRITORIAL CLAIMS

Kilometres   SCALE
0   400   800

Chile also claims land between
90° W. and 53° W. Argentina
claims land between 74° W.
and 25° W.

South Pole

PACIFIC OCEAN
ATLANTIC OCEAN
INDIAN OCEAN

WEDDELL SEA
ROSS SEA
SCOTIA SEA
TASMAN SEA

Bellingshausen Sea
Amundsen Sea
Davis Sea
Vincennes Bay
Porpoise Bay
Pine Island Gulf
Prydz Bay
Lützow-Holm Bay

GRAHAM LAND
ELLSWORTH LAND
MARIE BYRD LAND
VICTORIA LAND
WILKES LAND
QUEEN MAUD LAND
ENDERBY LAND
KEMP LAND
MAC-ROBERTSON LAND
PRINCESS ELIZABETH LAND
QUEEN MARY LAND
KAISER WILHELM II LAND
PALMER PENINSULA

ELLSWORTH MTS.
FILCHNER ICE SHELF
ROSS ICE SHELF
Permanent Ice Shelf
Polar Ice

Berkner I.
Alexander I.
Adelaide I.
Roosevelt I.
Ross I.
Balleny Is.
Berkner I.

× Sanae
× Lazarev
× Mawson
× Davis
× Mirnyy
× Vostok
× Byrd Station
× Little America
× Dumont d'Urville
× Palmer Station

(UNITED KINGDOM)
(NORWAY)
(AUSTRALIA)
(AUSTRALIA)
(NEW ZEALAND)
ADÉLIE LAND (FRANCE)

Antarctic Circle
Polar Ice

ARGENTINA
CHILE
Falkland Islands (Br.)
South Georgia I.
South Sandwich Is.
South Orkney Is.
South Shetland Is.
Prince Edward I. (S.Afr.)
Crozet Is. (Fr.)

Drake Passage
Bransfield Str.

Macquarie I. (Aust.)
Campbell I. (N.Z.)
Auckland Is. (N.Z.)
Antipodes Is.
Dunedin
NEW ZEALAND
Hobart
TASMANIA
Melbourne
AUSTRALIA

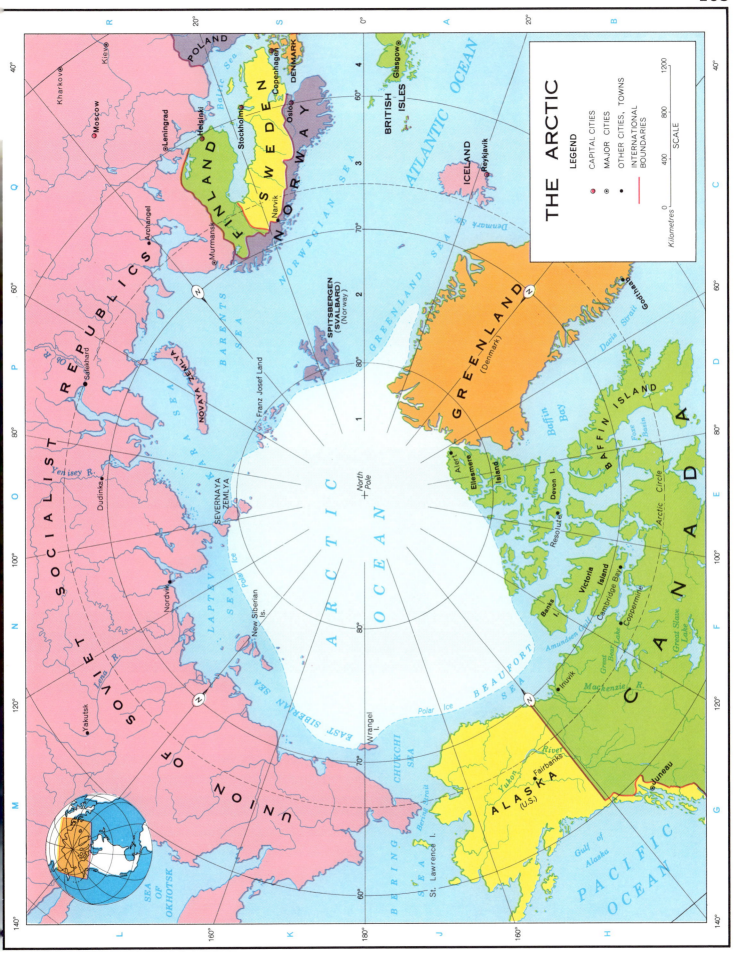

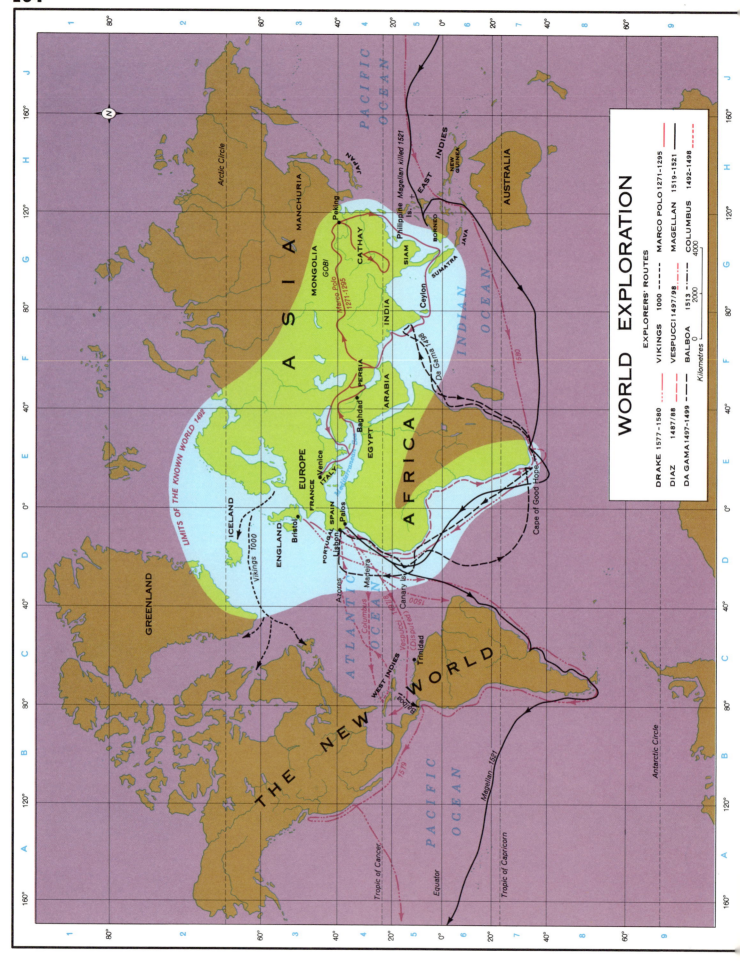

WORLD EXPLORATION

EXPLORERS' ROUTES

DRAKE 1577-1580	VIKINGS 1000	MARCO POLO 1271-1295
DIAZ 1487/88	VESPUCCI 1497/98	MAGELLAN 1519-1521
DA GAMA 1497-1499	BALBOA 1513	COLUMBUS 1492-1498

Kilometres
0   2000   4000

PACIFIC OCEAN

Arctic Circle

MANCHURIA

A S I A

MONGOLIA

GOBI

Peking

CATHAY

Marco Polo 1271-1295

JAPAN

EAST INDIES

NEW GUINEA

Philippine Magellan killed 1521
Is. +

Borneo

SIAM

SUMATRA

JAVA

AUSTRALIA

Ceylon

INDIA

PERSIA

Baghdad

ARABIA

EGYPT

Da Gama 1498

INDIAN OCEAN

1580

AFRICA

EUROPE

Venice

ITALY

FRANCE

PORTUGAL SPAIN

Lisbon Palos

Bristol

ENGLAND

ICELAND

Vikings 1000

LIMITS OF THE KNOWN WORLD 1492

GREENLAND

Azores

Madeira

Canary Is.

Columbus 1492

Vespucci (Disputed)

1500

ATLANTIC OCEAN

WEST INDIES

Trinidad

Balboa

T H E   N E W   W O R L D

Cape of Good Hope

1579

Magellan 1521

PACIFIC OCEAN

Tropic of Cancer

Equator

Tropic of Capricorn

Antarctic Circle

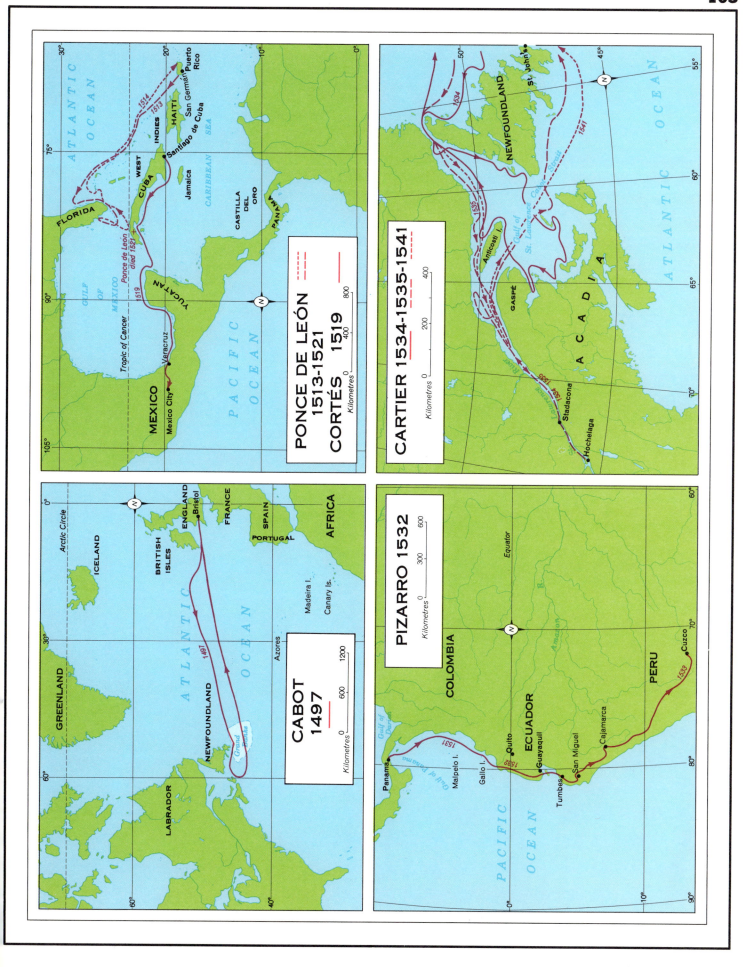

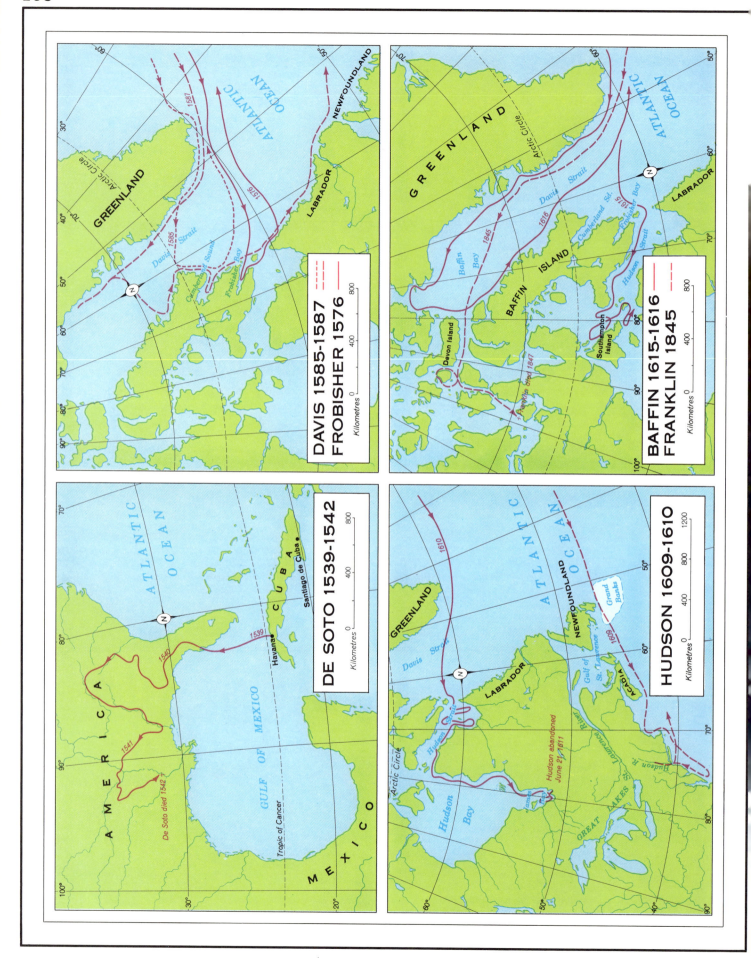

DAVIS 1585-1587
FROBISHER 1576

BAFFIN 1615-1616
FRANKLIN 1845

DE SOTO 1539-1542

HUDSON 1609-1610

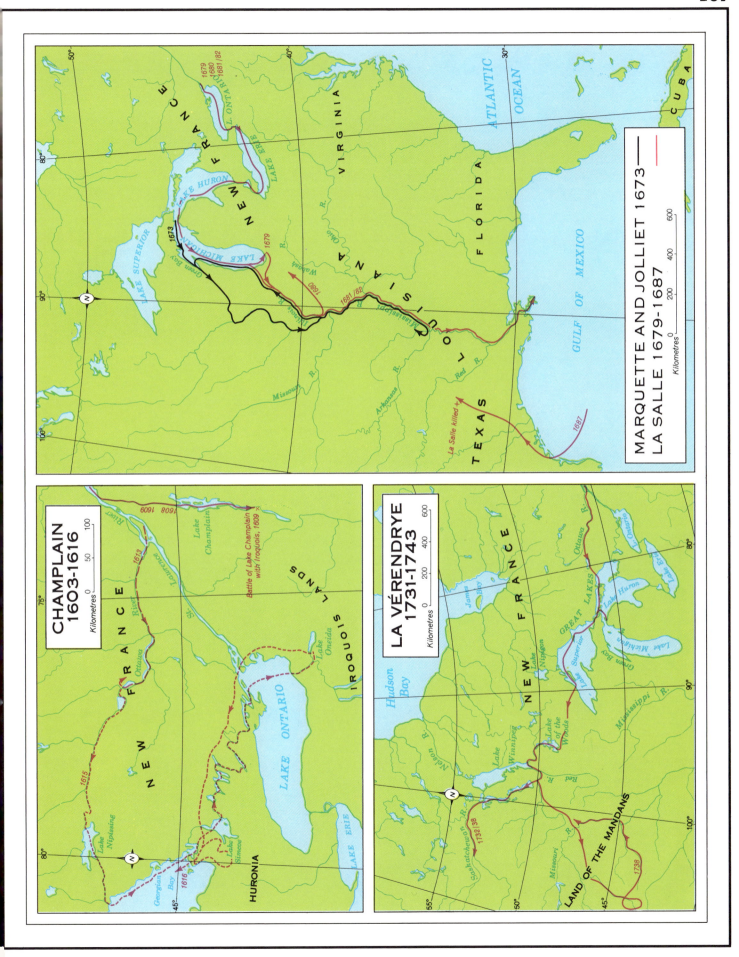

MARQUETTE AND JOLLIET 1673
LA SALLE 1679-1687

NEW FRANCE

VIRGINIA

LOUISIANA

FLORIDA

ATLANTIC OCEAN

CUBA

GULF OF MEXICO

TEXAS

La Salle killed +

1687

Kilometres
0 200 400 600

LAKE SUPERIOR
LAKE HURON
LAKE MICHIGAN
Green Bay
Illinois River
L. ONTARIO
LAKE ERIE
Wabash R.
Ohio R.
Missouri R.
Arkansas R.
Red R.
Mississippi R.

1679 1680 1681/82
1673
1679
1680
1681/82
1681/82

CHAMPLAIN 1603-1616

Kilometres
0 50 100

NEW FRANCE

Ottawa River
St. Lawrence River
Lake Champlain
Battle of Lake Champlain with Iroquois, 1609

IROQUOIS LANDS

Lake Oneida
LAKE ONTARIO
LAKE ERIE

Lake Nipissing
Georgian Bay
Lake Simcoe

HURONIA

1608/1609
1613
1615
1616

75°
80°
45°

LA VÉRENDRYE 1731-1743

Kilometres
0 200 400 600

NEW FRANCE

Hudson Bay
James Bay
Ottawa R.
L. Ontario
Lake Huron
Lake Michigan
Green Bay
GREAT LAKES
Lake Superior
Lake Nipigon
Lake of the Woods
Lake Winnipeg
Nelson R.
Saskatchewan R.
Red R.
Missouri R.
Mississippi R.

LAND OF THE MANDANS

1732/38
1738

90°
100°
55°
50°
45°

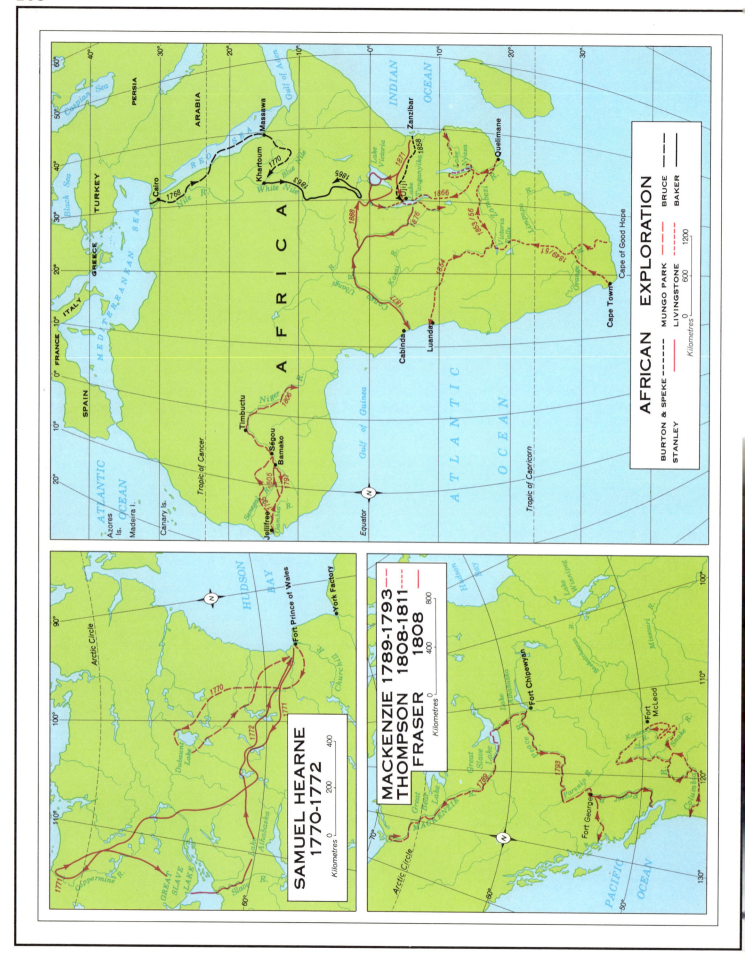

AFRICAN EXPLORATION

BURTON & SPEKE	MUNGO PARK	BRUCE
STANLEY	LIVINGSTONE	BAKER

Kilometres
0   600   1200

SAMUEL HEARNE
1770-1772

Kilometres
0   200   400

MACKENZIE 1789-1793
THOMPSON 1808-1811
FRASER 1808

Kilometres
0   400   800

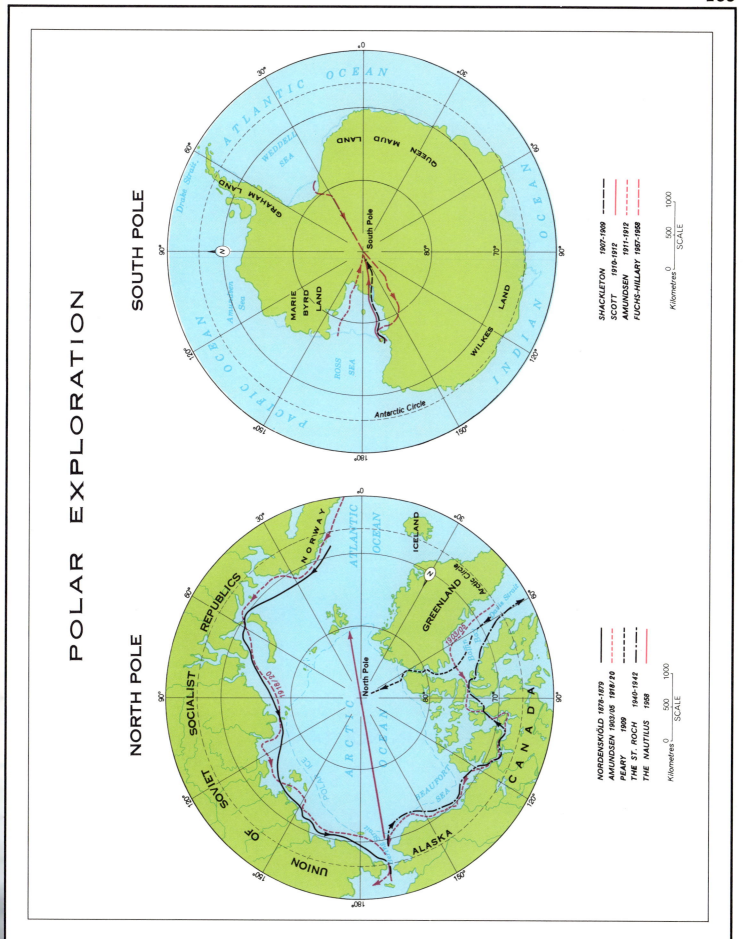

POLAR EXPLORATION

NORTH POLE

SOUTH POLE

NORDENSKIÖLD 1878-1879
AMUNDSEN 1903/05 1918/20
PEARY 1909
THE ST. ROCH 1940-1942
THE NAUTILUS 1958

SHACKLETON 1907-1909
SCOTT 1910-1912
AMUNDSEN 1911-1912
FUCHS-HILLARY 1957-1958

Kilometres 0 500 1000
SCALE

Kilometres 0 500 1000
SCALE

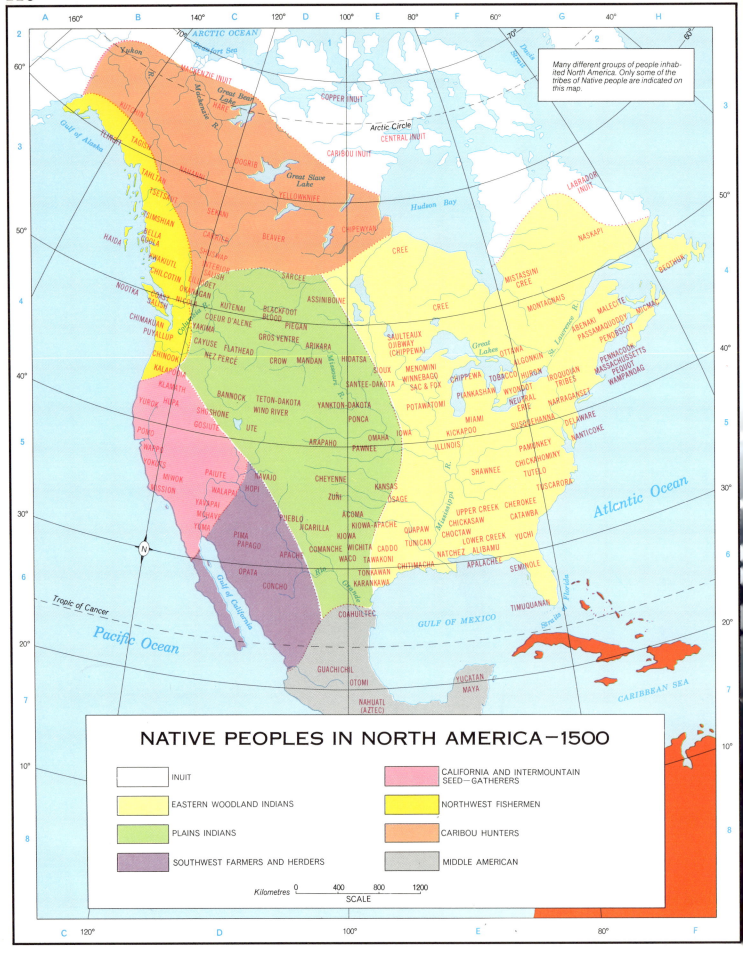

NATIVE PEOPLES IN NORTH AMERICA—1500

Many different groups of people inhabited North America. Only some of the tribes of Native people are indicated on this map.

INUIT	CALIFORNIA AND INTERMOUNTAIN SEED—GATHERERS
EASTERN WOODLAND INDIANS	NORTHWEST FISHERMEN
PLAINS INDIANS	CARIBOU HUNTERS
SOUTHWEST FARMERS AND HERDERS	MIDDLE AMERICAN

Kilometres 0 400 800 1200
SCALE

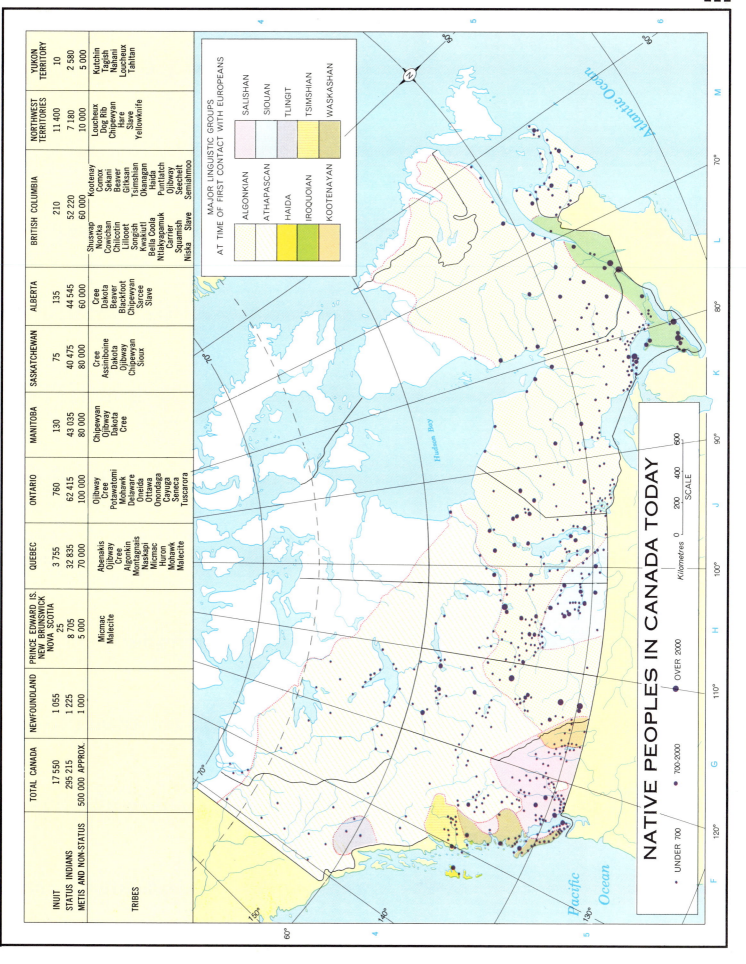

NATIVE PEOPLES IN CANADA TODAY

	TOTAL CANADA	NEWFOUNDLAND	PRINCE EDWARD IS. NEW BRUNSWICK NOVA SCOTIA	QUEBEC	ONTARIO	MANITOBA	SASKATCHEWAN	ALBERTA	BRITISH COLUMBIA	NORTHWEST TERRITORIES	YUKON TERRITORY
INUIT	17 550	1 055		3 755	760	130	75	135	210	11 400	10
STATUS INDIANS	295 215	1 225	8 705	32 835	62 415	43 035	40 475	44 545	52 220	7 180	2 580
METIS AND NON-STATUS	500 000 APPROX.	1 000	5 000	70 000	100 000	80 000	80 000	60 000	60 000	10 000	5 000
TRIBES			Micmac Malecite	Abenakis Ojibway Cree Algonkin Montagnais Naskapi Micmac Huron Mohawk Malecite	Ojibway Cree Potawatomi Mohawk Delaware Oneida Ottawa Onondaga Cayuga Seneca Tuscarora	Chipewyan Ojibway Dakota Cree	Cree Assiniboine Dakota Ojibway Chipewyan Sioux	Cree Dakota Beaver Blackfoot Chipewyan Sarcee Slave	Shuswap Nootka Cowichan Chilcotin Lillooet Songish Kwakiutl Bella Coola Ntlakyapamuk Carrier Squamish Niska Slave	Kootenay Comox Sekani Beaver Gitksan Tsimshian Okanagan Haida Puntlatch Ojibway Seechelt Semiahmoo	Loucheux Dog Rib Chipewyan Hare Slave Yellowknife	Kutchin Tagish Nahani Loucheux Tahltan

MAJOR LINGUISTIC GROUPS
AT TIME OF FIRST CONTACT WITH EUROPEANS

ALGONKIAN
ATHAPASCAN
HAIDA
IROQUOIAN
KOOTENAYAN

SALISHAN
SIOUAN
TLINGIT
TSIMSHIAN
WASKASHAN

SCALE
Kilometres 0 200 400 600

UNDER 700
700–2000
OVER 2000

Atlantic Ocean

Pacific Ocean

Hudson Bay

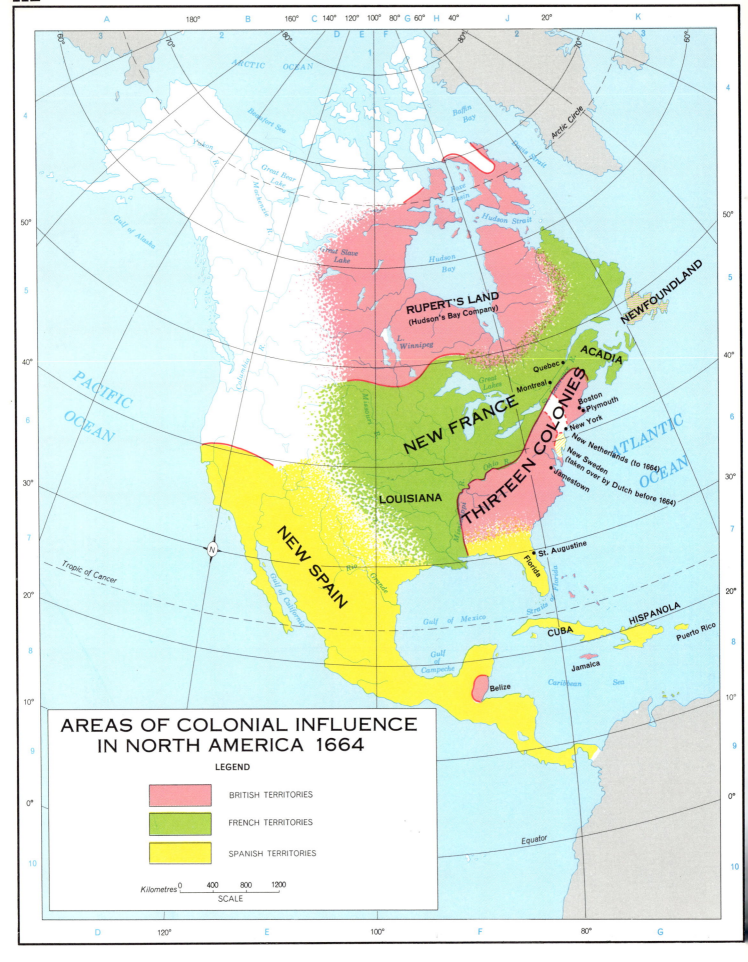

AREAS OF COLONIAL INFLUENCE
IN NORTH AMERICA 1664

LEGEND

▮	BRITISH TERRITORIES
▮	FRENCH TERRITORIES
▮	SPANISH TERRITORIES

Kilometres 0 400 800 1200
SCALE

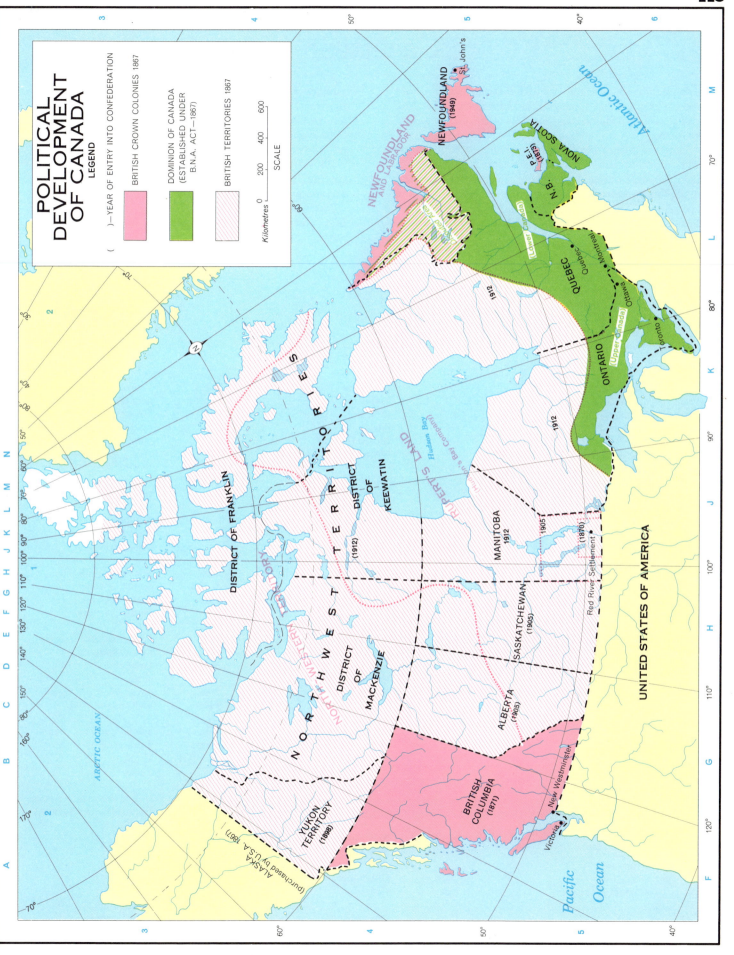

POLITICAL
DEVELOPMENT
OF CANADA

LEGEND

BRITISH CROWN COLONIES 1867

DOMINION OF CANADA
(ESTABLISHED UNDER
B.N.A. ACT—1867)

BRITISH TERRITORIES 1867

( )—YEAR OF ENTRY INTO CONFEDERATION

SCALE
Kilometres 0   200   400   600

Atlantic Ocean

NEWFOUNDLAND
AND LABRADOR

St. John's
NEWFOUNDLAND
(1949)

P.E.I.
(1873)

NOVA SCOTIA

N.B.

Lower Canada

QUEBEC
Quebec
Montreal

Upper Canada
Ottawa

ONTARIO
Toronto

1912

Hudson's Bay Company

Hudson Bay

RUPERT'S LAND

DISTRICT
OF
KEEWATIN

1912

N O R T H W E S T E R N   T E R R I T O R I E S

DISTRICT OF FRANKLIN

(1912)

NORTHWESTERN TERRITORY

DISTRICT
OF
MACKENZIE

MANITOBA
1912

1905

(1870)
Red River Settlement

SASKATCHEWAN
(1905)

ALBERTA
(1905)

UNITED STATES OF AMERICA

YUKON
TERRITORY
(1898)

ALASKA
(purchased by U.S.A. 1867)

BRITISH
COLUMBIA
(1871)

New Westminster

Victoria

ARCTIC OCEAN

Pacific
Ocean

Gazetteer

On the following pages are two alphabetical lists of all the important names that appear on the maps in this atlas. The first list is of Canadian names, and the other is of the rest of the world.

Names are generally followed by the name of the country, continent, or ocean in which they are situated. The Canadian names, however, are not followed by the name of the country, but they do include the name of the province in which the place is found. Those names that appear more than once are indexed only once, to the map on which they are most easily located.

After each name there is a figure that shows the page number of the map on which you will find the place. Following this is a letter and another figure. These refer to the letters along the top and bottom of each map and to the figures along each side. Together they will help you find the position of any place on the map.

Physical features as well as places are listed in the gazetteer. Each feature named is followed by a term indicating its nature, and abbreviated as shown below.

Names appearing more than once are listed in this order: first, place names; second, political divisions; and third, physical features.

Abbreviations

Afghan.	Afghanistan	Hon.	Honduras	P.E.I.	Prince Edward Island
Ala.	Alabama	*i., is.,* Is.	island(s)	*pen.*	peninsula
Alsk.	Alaska	Ill.	Illinois	Port.	Portuguese
Alta.	Alberta	*in.*	inlet	*prov.*	province
Antarc.	Antarctica	Ind. Oc.	Indian Ocean	*pt.*	point
arch.	archipelago	*isth.*	isthmus		
Arc. Oc.	Arctic Ocean			Que.	Quebec
Ariz.	Arizona	*l.,* **L.,** *ls.*	lake(s)		
At. Oc.	Atlantic Ocean	Louis.	Louisiana	*r.*	river
Aust.	Australia			*reg.*	region
		Man.	Manitoba	*rep.,* Rep.	republic
b.	bay	Mass.	Massachusetts	*res.*	reservoir
bas.	basin	Md.	Maryland	*res. stat.*	research station
B.C.	British Columbia	Med. S.	Mediterranean Sea		
		Mex.	Mexico	*s.,* S.	sea, Sea; South
c.	cape	Mich.	Michigan	S. Am.	South America
Calif.	California	Minn.	Minnesota	Sask.	Saskatchewan
C.A.R.	Central African Republic	Miss.	Mississippi	S.C.	South Carolina
		mt., **Mt.,** *mts.*	mountain(s)	*sd.*	sound
C. Am.	Central America			S. D.	South Dakota
Can.	Canada	N.	North, Northern; New	Sp.	Spain, Spanish
Carib. S.	Caribbean Sea	N. Am.	North America	St., Ste.	Saint(e)
ch.	channel	N.B.	New Brunswick	*str.*	strait
Congo Rep.	Congo Republic	N.C.	North Carolina	S.W.	South West
Conn.	Connecticut	N.D.	North Dakota	Switz.	Switzerland
cur.	current	Neb.	Nebraska		
Czech.	Czechoslovakia	Neth.	Netherlands	Tas.	Tasmania
		Nfld.	Newfoundland	Tenn.	Tennessee
Dem.	Democratic	N.H.	New Hampshire	*terr.,* Terr.	territory
Den.	Denmark	Nic.	Nicaragua	Tex.	Texas
des.	desert	N.J.	New Jersey		
dist.	district	N. Mex.	New Mexico	U.S.A.	United States of America
Dom. Rep.	Dominican Republic	N.S.	Nova Scotia	U.S.S.R.	Union of Soviet Socialist
		N.W.T.	Northwest Territories		Republics
Eur.	Europe	N.Y.	New York		
		N.Z.	New Zealand	Venez.	Venezuela
f.	feature				
Fla.	Florida	Okla.	Oklahoma	W.	West
Fr.	France, French	Ont.	Ontario	Wash.	Washington
				W. Virg.	West Virginia
g.	gulf	Pa.	Pennsylvania		
G. of Mex.	Gulf of Mexico	Pac. Oc.	Pacific Ocean	Zimb.	Zimbabwe
Guat.	Guatemala	Pak.	Pakistan		

Canada

Aberdeen, *l.*, N.W.T.	83 E3
Abitibi, *l.*, Ont./Que.	64 E3
Abitibi, *r.*, Ont.	64 D2
Aiyanish, B.C.	79 C1
Akimiski, *i.*, N.W.T.	83 E4
Aklavik, N.W.T.	83 C3
Akpatok, *i.*, N.W.T.	56 D1
Albany, *r.*, Ont.	64 D2
Albert, N.B.	51 C3
Alberta, *prov.*	40 G4
Alert, N.W.T.	83 F1
Alsask, Sask.	71 E5
Altona, Man.	67 D6
Amadjuak, *l.*, N.W.T.	83 F3
Amery, Man.	67 E2
Amherst, N.S.	51 C3
Amherstburg, Ont.	60 A3
Amisk, *l.*, Sask.	71 H3
Amundsen, *g.*, N.W.T.	44 F2
Annapolis, *r.*, N.S.	51 C3
Annapolis Royal, N.S.	51 C3
Annapolis Valley, N.S.	52 C3
Anticosti, *i.*, Que.	56 E4
Antigonish, N.S.	51 E3
Arctic, *arch.*	42 G2
Arctic Bay, N.W.T.	83 E2
Arctic Ocean	44 C2
Arctic Red River, N.W.T.	83 C3
Argentia, Nfld.	48 E4
Arnprior, Ont.	60 D2
Arrow, *ls.*, B.C.	79 E2
Arvida, Que.	56 C4
Assiniboia, Sask.	71 G6
Assiniboine, *r.*, Sask./Man.	67 B5
Athabasca, Alta.	75 F3
Athabasca, *l.*, Alta./Sask.	44 H4
Athabasca, *r.*, Alta.	44 G4
Athabasca Tar Sands, Alta.	78 G2
Atikokan, Ont.	64 B3
Atlantic Ocean	34 G6
Atlin, B.C.	79 B1
Atlin, *l.*, B.C./Yukon	79 B1
Attawapiskat, *r.*, Ont.	64 C2
Avalon, *pen.*, Nfld.	49 E4
Axel Heiberg, *i.*, N.W.T.	40 J2
Babine, *l.*, B.C.	79 C2
Back, *r.*, N.W.T.	83 D3
Baffin, *b.*, N.W.T.	44 M2
Baffin, *i.*, N.W.T.	40 L3
Bagotville, Que.	56 C4
Baie Comeau, Que.	56 D4
Baker Lake, N.W.T.	83 E3
Bancroft, Ont.	60 D2
Banff, Alta.	75 E5
Banks, *i.*, N.W.T.	40 F2
Barkerville, B.C.	82 D2
Barrie, Ont.	60 C2
Bathurst, N.B.	51 C2
Bathurst, *c.*, N.W.T.	83 C2
Bathurst, *i.*, N.W.T.	40 J2
Bathurst Inlet, N.W.T.	83 D3
Battle, *r.*, Alta.	75 G4
Battleford, Sask.	71 E4
Battle Harbour, Nfld.	40 N4

Bauld, *c.*, Nfld.	48 D2
Bay d'Espoir, Nfld.	50 D4
Bay of Islands, Nfld.	48 B3
Beardmore, Ont.	64 C3
Beatton River, B.C.	79 D1
Beaufort, *s.*	44 D2
Beauharnois, Que.	84 Map 2
Beauharnois, *canal.*, Que.	84 Map 2
Beausejour, Man.	67 D5
Beaver, *r.*, Sask.	71 E3
Becher, Ont.	63 B3
Belcher, *is.*, N.W.T.	83 F4
Bell, *i.*, Nfld.	48 D2
Bella Coola, B.C.	79 C2
Belle Isle, *i.*, Nfld.	48 D2
Belle Isle, *str.*, Nfld.	48 C2
Belleville, Ont.	60 D2
Berens, *r.*, Man.	67 D4
Berens River, Man.	67 D4
Biggar, Sask.	71 E4
Big Sand, *l.*, Man.	67 C2
Birch, *mts.*, Alta.	76 F2
Bishop's Falls, Nfld.	48 D3
Bissett, Man.	67 E5
Bistcho, *l.*, Alta.	75 C1
Blind River, Ont.	64 D3
Bloodvein, *r.*, Man.	67 E5
Boissevain, Man.	67 B6
Bonavista, Nfld.	48 E3
Bonavista, *b.*, Nfld.	48 E3
Bonne, *b.*, Nfld.	48 C3
Bonnyville, Alta.	78 G3
Boothia, *g.*, N.W.T.	44 K3
Boothia, *pen.*, N.W.T.	40 J2
Borden, P.E.I.	51 D2
Botwood, Nfld.	48 D3
Bow, *r.*, Alta.	75 F5
Bracebridge, Ont.	60 C2
Bralorne, B.C.	82 D2
Brampton, Ont.	60 C3
Brandon, Man.	67 C6
Brantford, Ont.	60 B3
Bras d'Or, *l.*, N.S.	51 E3
Bridgewater, N.S.	51 C3
British Columbia, *prov.*	40 F4
Brockville, Ont.	60 E2
Broughton Island, N.W.T.	83 F3
Buchans, Nfld.	48 C3
Buffalo Head Hills, *f.*, Alta.	76 D2
Burin, Nfld.	48 D4
Burin, *pen.*, Nfld.	49 D4
Burlington, Nfld.	48 D3
Burlington, Ont.	60 C3
Burntwood, *r.*, Man.	67 C3
Bylot, *i.*, N.W.T.	83 F2
Cabonga, *res.*, Que.	56 B4
Cabot, *str.*, N.S./Nfld.	44 N5
Caledonia, Ont.	63 C3
Caledonian Hills, N.B.	52 C3
Calgary, Alta.	75 E5
Cambridge, Ont.	60 B3
Cambridge Bay, N.W.T.	40 H3
Campbell River, B.C.	82 C2
Campbellton, N.B.	51 B2

Camrose, Alta.	75 F4
Canadian Shield, *f.*	35 F4
Canairiktok, *r.*, Nfld.	56 E3
Caniapiscau, *r.*, Que.	57 D2
Canso, N.S.	51 E3
Canso, *str.*, N.S.	51 E3
Cape Breton, *i.*, N.S.	51 E2
Cape Breton Highlands, N.S.	52 E2
Cape Dorset, N.W.T.	75 F3
Cape Tormentine, N.B.	51 D2
Carberry, Man.	67 C6
Carbonear, Nfld.	48 E4
Carcross, Yukon	83 C3
Cardinal, Ont.	84 Map 2
Cariboo, *mts.*, B.C.	80 D2
Caribou, *mts.*, Alta.	76 E1
Caribou, *r.*, Man.	67 E1
Carleton Place, Ont.	62 D2
Carlyle, Sask.	71 H6
Carmacks, Yukon	83 C3
Carrot, *r.*, Sask./Man.	71 H4
Cascade, *mts.*, B.C.	80 D3
Cassiar, B.C.	82 C1
Cassiar, *mts.*, B.C.	80 C1
Cedar, *l.*, Man.	67 C4
Chaleur, *b.*, Que.	56 D4
Channel – Port-aux-Basques, Nfld.	48 B4
Chapleau, Ont.	64 D3
Charlottetown, P.E.I.	51 D2
Charlton, *i.*, N.W.T.	65 E2
Chateauguay, *r.*, Que.	84 Map 2
Chatham, N.B.	51 C2
Chatham, Ont.	60 A3
Chaudière, *r.*, Que.	59 C2
Cheecham Hills, *f.*, Alta.	76 G3
Chesterfield Inlet, N.W.T.	83 E3
Chibougamau, Que.	56 C4
Chic-Chocs, *mts.*, Que.	57 D4
Chicoutimi, Que.	56 C4
Chidley, *c.*, Nfld.	56 E1
Chignecto, *b.*, N.S.	51 C3
Chilcotin, *r.*, B.C.	79 D2
Chilliwack, B.C.	79 D3
Chipman, N.B.	51 C2
Chippawa, Ont.	84 Map 1
Churchill, Man.	67 E1
Churchill, *c.*, Man.	67 F1
Churchill, *r.*, Nfld.	56 E3
Churchill, *r.*, Sask./Man.	44 J4
Churchill Falls, Nfld.	56 E3
Claire, *l.*, Alta.	75 F1
Claresholm, Alta.	75 F5
Clarkson, Ont.	63 C3
Clear Hills, *f.*, Alta.	76 C2
Clyde, N.W.T.	83 F2
Coast, *mts.*, B.C.	80 B1
Coats, *i.*, N.W.T.	83 E3
Cobalt, Ont.	64 E3
Cobequid, *mts.*, N.S.	52 D3
Cobourg, Ont.	60 C3
Cochrane, Ont.	64 D3
Cochrane, *r.*, Sask./Man.	67 B1
Cockburn, *i.*, Ont.	60 A2
Cold, *l.*, Alta./Sask.	75 G3
Coleville, Sask.	74 E5

Hearst, Ont.	64	D3
Hebron, Nfld.	56	E2
Hecate, *str.*, B.C.	79	B2
Henrietta Maria, *c.*, Ont.	64	D1
Herbert, Sask.	71	F5
Hermitage, Nfld.	48	D4
Hermitage, *b.*, Nfld.	48	C4
High River, Alta.	75	F5
High Rock, *l.*, Man.	67	B3
Hines Creek, Alta.	79	E1
Hodgson, Man.	67	D5
Holland, *r.*, Ont.	60	C2
Holman, N.W.T.	83	D2
Hope, B.C.	79	D3
Hope, *mts.*, Nfld.	57	E3
Hopedale, Nfld.	56	E2
Hopes Advance, *c.*, Que.	56	D1
Hubbart, *pt.*, Man.	67	E1
Hudson, *b.*	44	K4
Hudson, *str.*	44	L3
Hudson Bay, Sask.	71	H4
Hudson Bay Lowlands, *f.*	35	F4
Hull, Que.	56	B4
Humber, *r.*, Nfld.	48	C3
Humber, *r.*, Ont.	60	C3
Humboldt, Sask.	71	G4
Huntsville, Ont.	60	C2
Hurd, *c.*, Ont.	60	B2
Huron, *l.*	44	K5
Igloolik, N.W.T.	83	E3
Inuvik, N.W.T.	83	C3
Inverness, N.S.	51	E2
Iroquois Falls, Ont.	64	D3
Island, *l.*, Man.	67	E4
Island Falls, Sask.	74	H3
Jacques Cartier Passage, *str.*	56	E4
James, *b.*	44	K4
Jasper, Alta.	75	C4
Joliette, Que.	56	C4
Jones, *c.*, Que.	56	B3
Juan de Fuca, *str.*, Can./U.S.A.	79	D3
Kamloops, B.C.	79	D2
Kamloops Plateau, *f.*, B.C.	80	D2
Kamsack, Sask.	71	J5
Kapuskasing, Ont.	64	D3
Kapuskasing, *r.*, Ont.	64	D3
Kawartha, *ls.*, Ont.	60	C2
Keewatin, *dist.*	40	J3
Keewatin, Ont.	64	B3
Kelowna, B.C.	79	E3
Kelsey Bay, B.C.	79	C2
Kelvington, Sask.	71	H4
Kenogami, *r.*, Ont.	64	C2
Keno Hill, Yukon	83	C3
Kenora, Ont.	64	B3
Kentville, N.S.	51	C3
Kerrobert, Sask.	74	E5
Kicking Horse Pass, B.C./Alta.	75	D5
Kimberley, B.C.	79	E3
Kincardine, Ont.	60	B2
Kindersley, Sask.	71	E5
Kingston, Ont.	60	D2
King William, *i.*, N.W.T.	40	J3
Kirkland Lake, Ont.	64	D3
Kississing, *l.*, Man.	68	B3
Kitchener, Ont.	60	B3

Kitimat, B.C.	79	C2
Knox, *c.*, B.C.	79	B2
Koksoak, *r.*, Que.	56	D2
Kootenay, *l.*, B.C.	79	E3
Kootenay, *r.*, B.C./U.S.A.	79	E3
Labrador, Nfld.	40	M4
Labrador, *cur.*, At. Oc.	37	H4
Labrador City, Nfld.	56	D3
Lac Allard, Que.	58	E3
Lac Brochet, Man.	69	B1
Lachine, *canal*, Que.	84	Map 2
Lac Ile à la Crosse, Sask.	71	F3
Lac la Biche, Alta.	75	G3
Lac la Martre, N.W.T.	83	D3
Lac la Ronge, *l.*, Sask.	44	H4
Lacombe, Alta.	75	F4
Lac Seul, Ont.	64	B2
La Grande Rivière, *r.*, Que.	56	B3
Lake Harbour, N.W.T.	83	F3
Lake of Bays, *l.*, Ont.	60	C2
Lake of the Woods, *l.*, Man./Ont.	65	B3
Lancaster, *sd.*, N.W.T.	44	K2
La Ronge, Sask.	45	H4
Last Mountain, *l.*, Sask.	71	G5
La Tuque, Que.	56	C4
Laurentians, *mts.*, Que.	57	C4
Leaf, *b.*, Que.	56	D2
Leaf, *r.*, Que.	56	C2
Leamington, Ont.	60	A3
Leduc, Alta.	78	F4
Lesser Slave, *l.*, Alta.	75	E3
Lethbridge, Alta.	75	F6
Lévis, Que.	56	C4
Lewisporte, Nfld.	48	D3
Liard, *r.*, B.C./N.W.T.	44	F4
Lièvre, R. du, *r.*, Que.	56	B4
Lillooet, B.C.	79	D2
Lindsay, Ont.	60	C2
Little Mecatina, *r.*, Que.	56	F3
Liverpool, N.S.	51	C3
Lloydminster, Alta./Sask.	71	E4
Lobstick, *l.*, *see* Smallwood, *res.*	56	D3
London, Ont.	60	B3
Long, *pt.*, Man.	67	C4
Long, *pt.*, Ont.	60	B3
Longlac, Ont.	64	C3
Long Range, *mts.*, Nfld.	49	C3
Long Sault, Ont.	84	Map 2
Louisbourg, N.S.	51	E3
Lunenburg, N.S.	51	C3
Lynn Lake, Man.	67	B2
M'Clintock, *ch.*, N.W.T.	83	D2
M'Clure, *str.*, N.W.T.	83	D2
Mackenzie, *dist.*, N.W.T.	40	G3
Mackenzie, *r.*, N.W.T.	83	C3
Mackenzie King, *i.*, N.W.T.	83	D2
McMurray, Alta.	67	C2
Madawaska, *r.*, Ont.	60	D2
Madoc, Ont.	63	D2
Magdalen, *i.*, Que.	51	E2
Mahone Bay, N.S.	51	C3
Main, *ch.*, Ont.	61	B2
Manicouagan, *l.*, Que.	59	D1
Manicouagan, *r.*, Que.	59	D1
Manitoba, *prov.*	40	J4

Manitoba, *l.*, Man.	67	C5
Manitoba Escarpment, Man.	68	B5
Manitoulin, *i.*, Ont.	60	A2
Mansel, *i.*, N.W.T.	83	F3
Maple Creek, Sask.	71	E6
Marathon, Ont.	64	C3
Marmora, Ont.	63	D2
Masset, B.C.	79	B2
Matane, Que.	56	D4
Mattagami, *r.*, Ont.	64	D2
Mattawa, Ont.	64	E3
Mayo, Yukon	83	C3
Meadow Lake, Sask.	71	E3
Mealy, *mts.*, Nfld.	57	E3
Medicine Hat, Alta.	75	G5
Meelpaeg, *l.*, Nfld.	48	C3
Megantic, Que.	56	C4
Melfort, Sask.	71	G4
Melville, Sask.	71	H5
Melville, *i.*, N.W.T.	40	G2
Melville, *l.*, Nfld.	56	F3
Melville, *pen.*, N.W.T.	40	K3
Michikamau, *l.*, *see* Smallwood, *res.*	56	E3
Michipicoten, *i.*, Ont.	64	C3
Midland, Ont.	60	C2
Milk, *r.*, Alta./U.S.A.	75	G6
Minas Basin, N.S.	51	C3
Minnedosa, Man.	67	C5
Minto, N.B.	54	B2
Mirabel, *airport*, Que.	56	C4
Miramichi, *b.*, N.B.	51	C2
Miramichi, *r.*, N.B.	51	B2
Missinaibi, *r.*, Ont.	64	D3
Mississagi, *r.*, Ont.	60	A1
Mississauga, Ont.	60	C3
Mississippi, *r.*, Ont.	60	D2
Mistassibi, *r.*, Que.	56	C4
Mistassini, *l.*, Que.	56	C3
Moisie, *r.*, Nfld.	56	D3
Molson, *l.*, Man.	67	D3
Moncton, N.B.	51	C2
Mont Joli, Que.	56	D4
Mont Laurier, Que.	56	B4
Montreal, Que.	56	C4
Montreal, *l.*, Sask.	71	G3
Moose, *l.*, Man.	67	B3
Moose, *r.*, Ont.	64	D2
Moose Factory, Ont.	64	D2
Moose Jaw, Sask.	71	G5
Moosonee, Ont.	64	D2
Morden, Man.	67	C6
Moresby, *i.*, B.C.	79	B2
Morpeth, Ont.	63	B3
Morrisburg, Ont.	60	E2
Mulgrave, N.S.	51	E3
Murdochville, Que.	59	E2
Murray Harbour, P.E.I.	51	D2
Muskoka, *ls.*, Ont.	60	C2
Nahanni Butte, N.W.T.	83	C3
Nanaimo, B.C.	79	D3
Naskaupi, *r.*, Nfld.	56	E3
Nass, *r.*, B.C.	79	C1
Nechako Plateau, *f.*, B.C.	80	C2
Neepawa, Man.	67	C5
Nejanilini, *l.*, Man.	69	D1
Nelson, B.C.	79	E3
Nelson, *r.*, Man.	67	D3

Rupert House, Que.	56	B3	
Sable, *c.*, N.S.	51	C4	
Sable, *i.*, At. Oc.	54	D3	
Sachigo, *r.*, Ont.	68	G3	
Sachs Harbour, N.W.T.	83	C2	
Sackville, N.B.	51	C3	
Saguenay, *r.*, Que.	57	C4	
St. Andrews, N.B.	51	B3	
St. Anthony, Nfld.	48	D2	
St. Augustin, *r.*, Que.	56	F3	
St. Boniface, Man.	67	D6	
St. Catharines, Ont.	60	C3	
St. Clair, *l.*, Can./U.S.A.	44	K5	
St. Clair, *r.*, Can./U.S.A.	60	A3	
St. Croix, *r.*, Can./U.S.A.	51	B3	
St. Francis, *c.*, Nfld.	48	E4	
St. Francis, *l.*, Ont./Que.	84 Map 2		
St. George, N.B.	51	B3	
St. George, *c.*, Nfld.	48	B3	
St. George's, Nfld.	48	B3	
St. George's, *b.*, Nfld.	48	B3	
St. Hyacinthe, Que.	56	C4	
St. Ignace, *i.*, Ont.	64	C3	
Saint John, N.B.	51	B3	
St. John, *b.*, Nfld.	48	C2	
St. John, *c.*, Nfld.	48	D3	
St. John, *l.*, Que.,	56	C4	
Saint John, *r.*, N.B.	51	B2	
St. John's, Nfld.	48	E4	
St. Joseph, *i.*, Ont.	60	A1	
St. Joseph, *l.*, Ont.	64	B2	
St. Lawrence, Nfld.	50	D4	
St. Lawrence, *g.*	44	M5	
St. Lawrence, *r.*, Ont./Que.	56	D4	
St. Lawrence Lowlands, *f.*	35	G5	
St. Leonard, N.B.	51	B2	
St. Louis, *l.*, Que.	84 Map 2		
St. Marguerite, *r.*, Que.	59	D1	
St. Martin, *l.*, Man.	68	C5	
St. Mary's, Ont.	63	B3	
St. Mary's, *b.*, Nfld.	48	E4	
St. Mary's, *b.*, N.S.	51	B3	
St. Mary's, *c.*, Nfld.	48	D4	
St. Maurice, *r.*, Que.	56	C4	
St. Paul, *r.*, Que.	48	C2	
St. Paul's, *b.*, Nfld.	48	C3	
St. Stephen, N.B.	51	B3	
St. Thomas, Ont.	60	B3	
Salmon, *r.*, N.B.	51	C2	
Sandspit, B.C.	79	B2	
Sandy, *l.*, Ont.	64	B2	
Sanikiluaq, N.W.T.	83	F4	
Sarnia, Ont.	60	A3	
Saskatchewan, *prov.*	40	H4	
Saskatchewan, *r.*, Sask./Man.	72	H4	
Saskatoon, Sask.	71	F4	
Saugeen, *r.*, Ont.	60	B2	
Sault Ste. Marie, Ont.	64	D3	
Schefferville, Que.	56	D3	
Schreiber, Ont.	64	C3	
Scott, *c.*, B.C.	79	C2	
Scugog, *l.*, Ont.	60	C2	
Seal, *r.*, Man.	67	D1	
Seal Cove, Nfld.	48	C3	
Selkirk, Man.	67	D5	
Selkirk, *mts.*, B.C.	80	E2	
Sept Iles, Que.	56	D3	
Severn, *r.*, Ont.	60	C2	
Shawinigan, Que.	56	C4	
Shediac, N.B.	51	C2	
Sheet Harbour, N.S.	53	D3	
Shelburne, N.S.	51	C4	
Shelburne, Ont.	60	B2	
Shellbrook, Sask.	71	F4	
Sherbrooke, Que.	56	C4	
Sherridon, Man.	67	B3	
Shippigan, N.B.	51	C2	
Shippigan, *i.*, N.B.	51	C2	
Shipshaw, *r.*, Que.	59	C2	
Shuswap, *l.*, B.C.	79	E2	
Simcoe, Ont.	60	B3	
Simcoe, *l.*, Ont.	60	C2	
Sioux Lookout, Ont.	64	B2	
Sipiwesk, *l.*, Man.	67	D3	
Skagway, B.C.	79	A1	
Skeena, *r.*, B.C.	79	C1	
Slave, *r.*, Alta./N.W.T.	75	G1	
Smallwood, *res.*, Nfld.	57	E3	
Smithers, B.C.	45	F4	
Smiths Falls, Ont.	60	E2	
Smoky, *r.*, Alta.	75	C3	
Smooth Rock Falls, Ont.	64	D3	
Smoothstone, *l.*, Sask.	71	F3	
Snowdrift, N.W.T.	83	D3	
Snow Lake, Man.	67	C3	
Somerset, *i.*, N.W.T.	40	J2	
Sorel, Que.	56	C4	
Soulanges, *canal*, Que.	84 Map 2		
Souris, Man.	67	B6	
Souris, P.E.I.	51	D2	
Souris, *r.*, Can./U.S.A.	68	B6	
Southampton, *i.*, N.W.T.	40	K3	
Southern Indian, *l.*, Man.	67	C2	
South Indian Lake, Man.	67	C2	
South Knife, *r.*, Man.	67	E1	
South Mountain, N.S.	52	C3	
South, *mt.*, N.S.	52	C3	
South Nahanni, *r.*, N.W.T.	83	C3	
S. Saskatchewan, *r.*, Alta./Sask.	71	E5	
Spence Bay, N.W.T.	83	E3	
Split, *l.*, Man.	67	D2	
Springdale, Nfld.	48	C3	
Springhill, N.S.	51	C3	
Squamish, B.C.	79	D3	
Squaw Rapids, Sask.	74	H4	
Stallworthy, *c.*, N.W.T.	83	E1	
Steep Rock Lake, Ont.	64	B3	
Steinbach, Man.	67	D6	
Stephenville, Nfld.	48	B3	
Stewart, *r.*, Yukon	83	C3	
Stikine, *r.*, B.C.	79	B1	
Stikine Plateau, *f.*, B.C.	80	B1	
Stony, *l.*, Man.	67	C1	
Stratford, Ont.	60	B3	
Sturgeon Falls, Ont.	64	E3	
Sudbury, Ont.	64	D3	
Sugluk, Que.	56	B1	
Summerside, P.E.I.	51	D2	
Superior, *l.*	44	K5	
Sussex, N.B.	51	C3	
Swan, *l.*, Man.	67	B4	
Swan Hills, *f.*, Alta.	76	E3	
Swan River, Man.	67	B4	
Swift Current, Sask.	71	F5	
Sydney, N.S.	51	E2	
Sydney Mines, N.S.	51	E2	
Tadoule, *l.*, Man.	67	C1	
Tadoussac, Que.	56	D4	
Tatnam, *c.*, Man.	67	G2	
Tazin, *l.*, Sask.	75	H1	
Telegraph Creek, B.C.	79	B1	
Teslin, Yukon	83	C3	
Teslin, *l.*, Yukon	44	A3	
Thames, *r.*, Ont.	60	B3	
Thelon, *r.*, N.W.T.	83	D3	
The Pas, Man.	67	B4	
Thessalon, Ont.	64	D3	
Thetford Mines, Que.	56	C4	
Thompson, Man.	67	D3	
Thompson, *r.*, B.C.	79	D2	
Thunder Bay, Ont.	64	C3	
Thunder Bay, Ont.	65	C3	
Thunder Hills, *f.*, Sask.	72	F3	
Tignish, P.E.I.	51	C2	
Tilt Cove, Nfld.	50	D3	
Timagami, *l.*, Ont.	64	D3	
Timiskaming, Que.	56	B4	
Timiskaming, *l.*, Ont./Que.	64	E3	
Timmins, Ont.	64	D3	
Tisdale, Sask.	71	H4	
Tobermory, Ont.	60	B2	
Tobin, *l.*, Sask.	71	H4	
Torngat, *mts.*, Nfld.	35	G4	
Toronto, Ont.	60	C3	
Trail, B.C.	79	E3	
Trent, *canal/r.*, Ont.	84		
Trenton, Ont.	60	D2	
Trinity, Nfld.	48	E3	
Trinity, *b.*, Nfld.	48	E4	
Trois Rivières, Que.	56	C4	
Trout, *l.*, Ont.	64	B2	
Trout Lake, N.W.T.	83	C3	
Truro, N.S.	51	D3	
Tuktoyaktuk, N.W.T.	83	C3	
Turner Valley, Alta.	75	E5	
Turtle, *mt.*, Man.	68	B6	
Twillingate, Nfld.	48	D3	
Ungava, *b.*, Que.	44	M4	
Ungava, *pen.*, Que.	57	C1	
Unity, Sask.	71	E4	
Uranium City, Sask.	71	E1	
Utikuma, *l.*, Alta.	75	E3	
Val d'Or, Que.	56	B4	
Valleyfield, Que.	56	C4	
Val Marie, Sask.	71	F6	
Vancouver, B.C.	79	D3	
Vancouver, *i.*, B.C.	79	C3	
Vegreville, Alta.	75	G4	
Vermilion, Alta.	67	C3	
Vernon, B.C.	79	E2	
Victoria, B.C.	79	D3	
Victoria, *i.*, N.W.T.	40	H2	
Ville Marie, Que.	56	B4	
Virden, Man.	67	B6	
Viscount Melville, *sd.*, N.W.T.	44	H2	
Wabasca, *r.*, Alta.	75	E2	
Wabush, Nfld.	56	D3	
Wainwright, Alta.	75	G4	
Walkerton, Ont.	60	B2	
Wallaceburg, Ont.	60	A3	
Waterhen, *l.*, Man.	68	C4	
Wathaman, *r.*, Sask.	71	G2	

The World

(EXCEPT CANADA)

124

125

Pôrto Velho, Brazil	90	C3
Port Said, Egypt	94	G2
Port Sudan, Sudan	94	G4
Portugal, Europe	96	C5
Potosí, Bolivia	90	C4
Prague, Czech.	96	E3
Pretoria, Rep. of S. Africa	94	F8
Prince Edward, is., Ind. Oc.	27	
Prince of Wales, i., Alsk., U.S.A.	79	B1
Princess Elizabeth Land, Antarc.	102	D2
Providence, Rhode I., U.S.A.	85	F2
Prydz., b., Ind. Oc.	102	D3
Puebla, Mex.	87	E4
Pueblo, Colorado, U.S.A.	85	C3
Puerto Barrios, Guat.	88	B1
Puerto Cortés, Hond.	88	B1
Puerto Rico, i., Carib. S.	89	E3
Punta Arenas, Chile	90	B8
Puntarenas, Costa Rica	88	C3
Pusan, S. Korea	98	G3
Pyongyang, N. Korea	98	G3
Pyrenees, mts., Sp./France	97	D4
Qatar, Asia	98	C3
Queen Mary Land, Antarc.	102	E2
Queen Maud Land, Antarc.	102	A2
Queensland, state, Aust.	100	D4
Quelimane, Mozambique	94	G7
Querétaro, Mex.	87	D3
Quezaltenango, Guat.	88	A2
Quezon City, Philippines	98	G4
Quito, Ecuador	90	B3
Rabat, Morocco	94	C2
Raleigh, N.C., U.S.A.	85	F3
Rangoon, Burma	98	E4
Rapid City, S.D., U.S.A.	85	C2
Raquette, r., U.S.A.	85 Map 2	
Rawalpindi, Pakistan	98	D3
Recife, Brazil	90	F3
Red, r., U.S.A./Can.	86	D2
Red, r., U.S.A.	86	D3
Red, s., Africa/Asia	94	G3
Reno, Nevada, U.S.A.	85	B3
Republic of South Africa, Africa	94	F9
Revillagigedo, i., Alsk., U.S.A.	79	B1
Reykjavik, Iceland	96	B2
Rheims, France	96	D4
Rhine, r., Europe	96	D3
Rhode Island, state, U.S.A.	85	F2
Rhodes, i., Med. S.	96	F5
Rhodesia, see Zimbabwe	94	F7
Rhône, r., France	96	D4
Richmond, Virginia, U.S.A.	85	F3
Riga, U.S.S.R.	96	F3
Rio Branco, Brazil	90	C3
Rio de Janeiro, Brazil	90	E5
Rio de la Plata, r., S. Am.	91	D6
Rio Grande, r., U.S.A./Mex.	86	C4
Rio Grande de Santiago, r., Mex.	87	D3
Riyadh, Saudi Arabia	98	C3
Roanoke, r., U.S.A.	86	F3
Rochester, N.Y., U.S.A.	60	D3
Rockhampton, Aust.	100	E4
Rocky, mts., U.S.A./Can.	86	B2

Romania, Europe	96	F4
Rome, Italy	96	E4
Roosevelt, i., Antarc.	102	K1
Rosario, Argentina	90	C6
Ross, i., Antarc.	102	J2
Ross, s., Pac. Oc.	102	K2
Ross Ice Shelf, f., Antarc.	102	K1
Rostov, U.S.S.R.	96	G4
Royale, i., U.S.A.	64	C3
Rub' al Khali, des., Saudi Arabia	99	C4
Rudolf, l., see Turkana, l.	94	G5
Rwanda, Africa	94	F6
Ryukyu, is., Pac. Oc.	98	G3
Sabah, i., Malaysia	98	F4
Sable, c., Fla., U.S.A.	85	E4
Sacramento, Calif., U.S.A.	85	A3
Sacramento, r., Calif., U.S.A.	86	A3
Saginaw, b., L. Huron	60	A3
Sagua la Grande, Cuba	89	B2
Sahara, des., Africa	95	E3
Saharan Atlas, mts., Africa	95	D2
Saigon, see Ho Chi Minh	98	F4
St. Clair, l., Canada/U.S.A.	85	E2
St. Clair, r., Canada/U.S.A.	60	A3
St. Croix, i., Carib. S.	89	F3
St. Helena, i., At. Oc.	95	C7
St. Kitts, i., Leeward Is.	89	F3
St. Lawrence, i., Bering S.	103	J3
St. Lawrence Lowlands, f., Canada/U.S.A.	35	G5
St. Louis, Missouri, U.S.A.	85	D3
St. Louis, Senegal	94	B4
St. Lucia, i., Windward Is.	89	F4
St. Marc, Haiti	89	D3
St. Martin, i., Carib. S.	89	F3
St. Paul, Minn., U.S.A.	85	D2
St. Pierre, i., At. Oc.	48	C4
St. Regis, r., U.S.A.	84 Map 2	
St. Thomas, i., Carib. S.	89	E3
St. Vincent, c., Portugal	96	C5
St. Vincent and the Grenadines, Windward Is.	89	F4
Sakhalin, i., U.S.S.R.	98	H2
Salekhard, U.S.S.R.	103	P3
Salem, Oregon, U.S.A.	85	A2
Salisbury, Zimbabwe	94	G7
Salonica, Greece	96	F4
Salt Lake City, Utah, U.S.A.	85	B2
Salton, s., Calif., U.S.A.	86	B3
Salvador, Brazil	90	F4
Salween, r., Burma/China	98	E3
Samoa, is., see Western Samoa	100	H3
San'a, Yemen	98	C4
Sanae, res. stat., Antarc.	102	S2
San Antonio, Tex., U.S.A.	85	D4
San Antonio, c., Cuba	89	B2
San Diego, Calif., U.S.A.	85	B3
San Francisco, Calif., U.S.A.	85	A3
San José, Costa Rica	88	C3
San Juan, Puerto Rico	89	E3
San Juan, r., Nic./Costa Rica	88	C2
San Juan del Sur, Nic.	88	B2
San Lucas, c., Mex.	87	C3
San Luis Potosí, Mex.	87	D3
San Miguel, El Salvador	88	B2
San Pedro Sula, Hon.	88	B1
San Salvador, El Salvador	88	B2

Santa Ana, El Salvador	88	B2
Santa Barbara, is., Calif.	86	B3
Santa Clara, Cuba	89	C2
Santa Cruz, Argentina	90	C8
Santa Eugenia, pt., Mex.	87	A2
Santa Fe, Argentina	90	C6
Santa Fe, N. Mex., U.S.A.	85	C3
Santa Rosa, Hon.	88	B2
Santiago, Chile	90	B6
Santiago, Panama	88	C3
Santiago de Cuba	89	C2
Santiago de los Caballeros, Dom. Rep.	89	D3
Santo Domingo, Dom. Rep.	89	E3
São Francisco, r., Brazil	90	E3
São Luis, Brazil	90	E3
São Paulo, Brazil	90	E5
São Roque, c., Brazil	90	F3
São Tomé e Principe, is., At. Oc.	94	D5
Sarawak, Malaysia	98	F4
Sardinia, i., Med. S.	96	D4
Saudi Arabia, Asia	98	C3
Sava, r., Yugoslavia	96	E4
Savannah, Georgia, U.S.A.	85	E3
Savannah, r., U.S.A.	86	E3
Scotia, s., At. Oc.	102	Q4
Scotland, Great Britain	96	C3
Seattle, Wash., U.S.A.	85	A2
Segovia, r., Hon./Nic.	88	B2
Seine, r., France	96	D4
Selvas, f., S. Am.	91	C3
Senegal, Africa	94	B4
Senegal, r., Africa	94	B4
Seoul, S. Korea	98	G3
Serowe, Botswana	94	F8
Severnaya Zemlya, is., U.S.S.R.	103	O2
Seville, Spain	96	C5
Seychelles, is., Ind. Oc.	27	
Shanghai, China	98	G3
Shenyang, China	98	G2
Shetland, is., At. Oc.	96	C2
Shikoku, i., Japan	98	G3
Shreveport, Louis., U.S.A.	85	D3
Siam, see Thailand	98	F4
Sian, China	98	F3
Sicily, i., Med. S.	96	E5
Sierra Leone, Africa	94	B5
Sierra Madre del Sur, mts., Mex.	87	D4
Sierra Madre Occidental, mts., Mex.	87	C2
Sierra Madre Orientale, mts., Mex.	87	D2
Sierra Nevada, mts., U.S.A.	86	A3
Si-Kiang, r., China	98	F3
Sikkim, India	98	E3
Singapore, Asia	98	F4
Sinkiang, prov., China	98	E2
Sioux Falls, S.D., U.S.A.	85	D2
Skagerrak, str., Norway/Denmark	96	D3
Skagway, Alsk., U.S.A.	79	A1
Snake, r., U.S.A.	86	B2
Socotra, i., Arabian Sea	98	C4
Sofia, Bulgaria	96	F4
Solomon, is., Pac. Oc.	100	E2
Somali, pen., Africa	95	H5

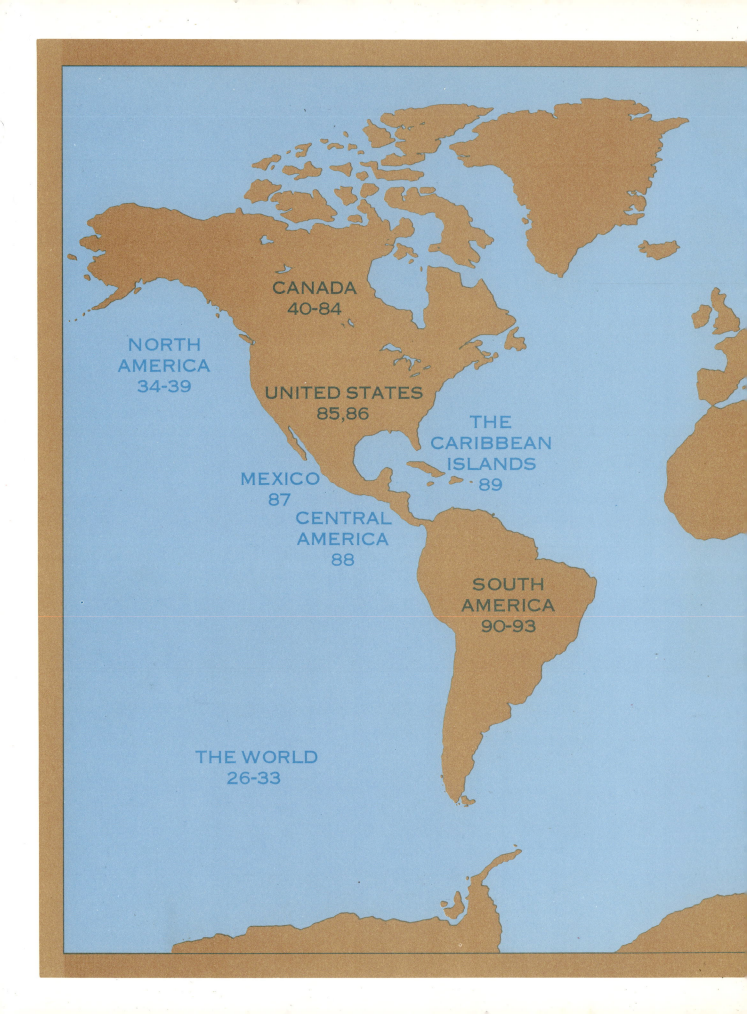